MW01120621

Professionalizing Public Relations

Kate Fitch

Professionalizing Public Relations

History, Gender and Education

HUMBER LIBRARIES LAKESHORE CAMPUS
3199 Lakeshore Blvd West
TORONTO, ON.   M8V 1K8

palgrave
macmillan

Kate Fitch
Murdoch University
Perth, Australia

ISBN 978-1-137-57308-7   ISBN 978-1-137-57309-4   (eBook)
DOI 10.1057/978-1-137-57309-4

Library of Congress Control Number: 2016948773

© The Editor(s) (if applicable) and The Author(s) 2016
The author(s) has/have asserted their right(s) to be identified as the author(s) of this work
in accordance with the Copyright, Designs and Patents Act 1988.
This work is subject to copyright. All rights are solely and exclusively licensed by the
Publisher, whether the whole or part of the material is concerned, specifically the rights of
translation, reprinting, reuse of illustrations, recitation, broadcasting, reproduction on
microfilms or in any other physical way, and transmission or information storage and retrieval,
electronic adaptation, computer software, or by similar or dissimilar methodology now
known or hereafter developed.
The use of general descriptive names, registered names, trademarks, service marks, etc. in this
publication does not imply, even in the absence of a specific statement, that such names are
exempt from the relevant protective laws and regulations and therefore free for general use.
The publisher, the authors and the editors are safe to assume that the advice and information
in this book are believed to be true and accurate at the date of publication. Neither the publisher nor the authors or the editors give a warranty, express or implied, with respect to the
material contained herein or for any errors or omissions that may have been made.

Printed on acid-free paper

This Palgrave Macmillan imprint is published by Springer Nature
The registered company is Macmillan Publishers Ltd. London

To Damian for his unstinting love and support

ACKNOWLEDGEMENTS

This book could not have been written without the support of many people. I am grateful to the scholars who offered feedback on early work, pointed me to relevant sources and scholarship, and encouraged me to write a book: Lee Edwards, Jan Gothard, Anne Gregory, Meg Lamme, Jacquie L'Etang, Alec McHoul, David McKie, Judy Motion, Magda Pieczka, Mark Sheehan, Anne Surma, Amanda Third, Kathryn Trees, Carol Warren, Tom Watson, and Sandra Wilson. I thank the 14 participants who responded positively to my interview requests and shared their experiences and personal records. In particular, I thank Marjorie Anderson for her preservation of National Education Committee archives. The Public Relations Institute of Australia supported this research though permission to cite from various archival collections related to their organization. I also acknowledge assistance provided by many archivists and librarians at Battye Library, Mitchell Library, State Library of New South Wales, State Library of Victoria, State Library of Western Australia, and University of New South Wales as well as the digitised newspaper archives available though Trove Australia. Finally, I thank Liz Barlow at Palgrave Macmillan for her enthusiastic response to my initial book proposal, Maddie Holder for editorial guidance and support, and Indra Priyadarshini for production management.

Parts of this book were originally published as journal articles. In addition, the links between feminization and professionalization were originally explored in a book chapter. I thank the publishers for permission to draw on that material in this book.

Reproduced by permission of Elsevier from Fitch, K. (2014). Professionalisation and public relations education: Industry accreditation of Australian university courses in the early 1990s. *Public Relations Review*, 40, 623–631. doi:10.1016/j.pubrev.2014.02.015.

Reproduced by permission of SAGE Publications Ltd., London, Los Angeles, New Delhi, Singapore and Washington DC, from Fitch, K. (2015). Making history: Reflections on memory and "elite" interviews in public relations research. *Public Relations Inquiry*, 4(2), 131–144. doi:10.1177/2046147X15580684 (© The Author, 2015).

Reproduced by permission of SAGE Publications Ltd., London, Los Angeles, New Delhi, Singapore and Washington DC, from Fitch, K. (2014). Perceptions of public relations education, 1985–1999. *Public Relations Inquiry*, 3(3), 271–291. doi:10.1177/2046147X14535398 (© The Author, 2014).

Fitch, K., & Third, A. (2014). Ex-journos and promo girls: Feminization and professionalization in the Australian public relations industry. In C. Daymon & K. Demetrious (Eds.), *Gender and public relations: Critical perspectives on voice, image and identity* (pp. 247–268). London, England: Routledge.

Fitch, K. (2013). A disciplinary perspective: The internationalization of Australian public relations education. *Journal of Studies in International Education*, 17(2), 136–147. doi:10.1177/1028315312474898© 2013 Nuffic. Reprinted by Permission of SAGE Publications, Inc.

CONTENTS

List of Abbreviations and Acronyms

ABS	Australian Bureau of Statistics
AIPR	Australian Institute of Public Relations
AJA	Australian Journalists Association (from 1992, Media Entertainment and Arts Alliance)
APBC	Australian Progressive Business College
BOAC	British Overseas Airways Corporation
CAMSA	Council of Australian Marketing Service Associations
ECU	Edith Cowan University
EWA	Eric White Associates
FPRIA	Fellow of the Public Relations Institute of Australia
IPR	Institute of Public Relations (UK)
IPRA	International Public Relations Association
IPRS	Institute of Public Relations Singapore
MPRIA	Member of the Public Relations Institute of Australia
NEC	National Education Committee
NSW	State of New South Wales
PRIA	Public Relations Institute of Australia
PRIA (Vic)	Public Relations Institute of Australia (Victoria)
PRSA	Public Relations Society of America
QIT	Queensland Institute of Technology
RMIT	Royal Melbourne Institute of Technology
QUT	Queensland University of Technology
UK	United Kingdom
US/USA	United States
UTS	University of Technology Sydney

WA   State of Western Australia
WACAE   Western Australian College of Advanced Education
WAIT   Western Australian Institute of Technology

INTRODUCTION

Public relations suffers from both semantic instability and confusion about its social legitimacy. Its supporters point to its essential role in modern democracy and position the occupation as an ethical business management practice seeking dialogue and engagement with key publics. Those supporters may be individual practitioners and institutions, such as professional associations, determined to claim professional recognition, or universities where public relations education offers a lucrative revenue stream. Its detractors—and there are many—deride public relations for its lack of ethics, links with propaganda, and manipulation of the masses. These detractors include journalists, for whom public relations is "the dark side" to which they may one day cross over. Critical scholars point to public relations' role in maintaining power among society's elites, particularly in government and corporate sectors. Further, public relations education is often criticized by industry representatives and by scholars in other disciplines who challenge its academic legitimacy.

Professionalizing Public Relations enters into a debate about how to make sense of these divergent perspectives. This book considers that much of what is understood about contemporary public relations stems from uncritical histories about its development to the modern era. Although its focus is the Australian public relations industry in the second half of the twentieth century, the findings are significant for public relations history and historiography globally. The book challenges understandings of public relations' history as an evolutionary progression towards a profession by considering the impact of societal and structural factors on the institutionalization of public relations and the constitution of public relations knowledge and expertise. That is, contrary to widely accepted historical narratives, public relations did not develop in a vacuum or as the result of the efforts of the field's (mostly male) heroes and professional associations.

Using archival research and interviews, *Professionalizing Public Relations* offers a critical investigation, and an alternative to the dominant Anglo-American and corporatist approaches to the field, in order to develop a new understanding of public relations history. It examines the broader social and political context that shaped the development of the public relations industry in Australia and considers previously unexplored themes such as the changing relationship between women and work and the massification of higher education in the final decades of the twentieth century. Situating this study within a broader context avoids relying on a narrow conceptualization of public relations activity and challenges existing and widely accepted histories of Australian public relations. It reveals attempts to establish professional recognition for the field, and, ultimately, the failure of a professional association to regulate public relations activity in Australia.

Conceptualizing Public Relations

The idea of a dominant paradigm for public relations was coined by Pieczka in 1994 (L'Etang, 2008a, 2009), who used it to describe primarily US public relations scholarship, which drew on management, organizational, and systems theories. It embraces functionalist and managerialist understandings of public relations, aiming for both organizational effectiveness and symmetrical practices to establish professional status and social legitimacy. In *Managing Public Relations*, Grunig and Hunt described public relations as "a young profession, which in the 1980s has only begun to approach true professional status" (1984, p. 4). Acknowledging that "the profession has its roots in press agentry and propaganda, activities that society generally holds in low esteem," they nonetheless argued that public relations had "made great strides in its sophistication, ethics, responsibility, and contribution to society" (Grunig & Hunt, 1984, p. 4). The authors presented public relations in terms of four models—press agentry, public information, two-way asymmetry, and two-way symmetry—to describe the historical development of public relations. L'Etang described these models as "responsible for the development of the major theoretical framework for the field" (2008a, p. 251) and McKie and Munshi identify Grunig and Hunt's book as "the seminal text of contemporary public relations" (2007, p. 12). As such, these models have fundamentally shaped understandings of public relations in industry, in education, and in scholarship.

In recent years, however, public relations scholars have begun to draw on diverse theoretical and disciplinary perspectives to challenge this paradigm. Many of these scholars are critical of its symmetrical approach to defining public relations as an ethical, effective management practice and a modern profession. Motion and Weaver (2005) argue that normative and functional approaches privilege organizational interests, fail to address inequalities in power, and ignore the social and political contexts of public relations practice. Significantly, the promotion of professional public relations as objective, value-free, and universal ignores the specific social context in which such ideas emerged (L'Etang, 2008a). Roper (2005) views symmetrical communication as a hegemonic practice used by powerful organizations to avoid criticism and maintain unequal power relations with their stakeholders. McKie and Munshi (2007) reject understandings of public relations as a management function or discipline, arguing that this approach positions the field only as a government or corporate function and ignores the full realm of public relations activities such as its use in activism and in non-government sectors. The focus on managerial, organizational, and functionalist perspectives in the dominant paradigm inevitably meant that many public relations scholars fail to consider the broader role of public relations in society (Edwards & Hodges, 2011; Ihlen & Verhoeven, 2009).

The challenges to normative and functional approaches by mostly non-US scholars are described by Edwards and Hodges (2011) as a socio-cultural turn in public relations scholarship (see also Ihlen & van Ruler, 2009). They call for more radical research to understand the influence of public relations on society and of society on public relations and argue that a focus on societal perspectives reframes mainstream understandings of public relations and allows different kinds of research, such as investigating how professional narratives privilege different kinds of knowledge, how public relations engages with different and dynamic socio-cultural contexts, and why the profession takes a particular form (Edwards & Hodges, 2011, pp. 6–8). *Professionalizing Public Relations* therefore seeks a critical understanding of the historical development of Australian public relations. This book contributes to the body of public relations scholarship investigating professionalization and sociology of the professions. Drawing on the work of critical scholars such as Lee Edwards, Jacquie

L'Etang, and Magda Pieczka, it considers public relations broadly as communicative practice, an occupation, and an industry in order to investigate the social structures and ideologies which underpin claims to professional recognition and the dynamic constitution of public relations knowledge and expertise.

INVESTIGATING PUBLIC RELATIONS HISTORY

Public relations history tends to be presented somewhat uncritically as a linear, progressive narrative of development, or, in the words of Lamme and Miller, as "a progressive evolution from unsophisticated and unethical early roots to planned, strategic, and ethical campaigns of the current day" (2010, p. 281). Lamme and Miller (2010) and L'Etang (2008b, 2014) attribute this steady development towards professional standing to the practice of colligation or periodization, that is, its organization or patterning into particular time periods to describe pivotal developmental phases as in the four models in the Grunigian paradigm. Pearson identifies the broad management paradigm that offers a structural–functional explanation for public relations as the most common and that it legitimates "organizational needs"; however, Pearson argues, this functionalist emphasis stems from public relations' role in serving "the needs of profit-making organizations in a post-industrial capitalist economy" (2009, p. 108). L'Etang (2014) maintains this particular colligation has ensured the dominance of US versions of the emergence and historical development of public relations. Indeed, US public relations histories tend to be dominated by business and politics, resulting in an almost exclusive focus on corporate public relations (L'Etang, 2004, 2008b; Miller, 2000; Myers, 2014).

Given the recent global interest in public relations history, spearheaded in part by the inaugural International Public Relations History Conference at Bournemouth University in 2010, and recent publications such as the National Perspectives on the Development of Public Relations: Other Voices book series (Watson, 2014–2015) and *Pathways to Public Relations: Histories of Practice and Profession* (St John III, Lamme, & L'Etang, 2014), there is growing recognition of the significance of progressivist and evolutionary historical accounts. Tom Watson, founder of the International Public Relations History Conference, identified the need for more critical histories and called for public relations historians to "be more dangerous," and to "avoid Grunigian analysis as an historiographic tool" (2013, p. 19). Drawing on Foucault (1972), critical histories problematize the way history is used. A critical approach is relevant for *Professionalizing Public Relations* because I am trying to understand the factors that shaped contemporary public relations in Australia. Rather than steady progress towards a modern profession, this book considers instead the ways in which the professional association understood the role of, and attempted to regulate, public relations activity and the significance for the ways in which public relations knowledge is constituted, contested, and institutionalized in the Australian context.

Few public relations histories consider historiography, that is, the construction of histories focusing on methodological conventions (L'Etang, 2016). Public relations histories are always written from certain ideological positions, which influence the interpretation and construction of those histories (Pearson, 2009). L'Etang likens the absence of historiography from the field to "the poor relation," arguing the tension between public relations as an occupational practice striving for professional recognition and broader public communication activity results in ontological issues (2015a, p. 73; 2016). The danger is that public relations history is confined to largely descriptive or highly subjective accounts of its development, with little reflexivity around source analysis, the subjectivity of the researcher, or the retrospective accounts offered by research participants.

Textbook histories and practitioner memoirs are not evidence-based but offer retrospective and reconstructed narratives of the past (Fitch, 2015). They attribute the post-World War II founding of a professional institute to the birth of modern public relations in Australia, thereby linking the history of the public relations industry in Australia closely with one professional association, the Public Relations Institute of Australia (PRIA) and the achievements of its senior members. These accounts perceive a significant debt to US practices, and understand World War II military information structures as pivotal in the development of the modern profession. In contrast, I consider the development of public relations in relation to broader societal structures and institutional processes, such as the expansion of the Australian higher education sector, the changing demographics of the workforce, and the global context for public relations activity. This book therefore offers an historical perspective on the development of public relations, focusing on the institutionalization and professionalization of Australian public relations. This historical research is significant because it seeks to understand how certain discourses around public relations became dominant and how particular social and historical contexts contributed to the constitution of a public relations body of knowledge in Australia.

Book Structure

This introduction outlines the scope of this book and identifies the need for more critical investigations of public relations history.

Chapter 1 offers a theoretical context for this study, drawing primarily on sociology of the professions. It explores the public relations industry's preoccupation with its professional status before considering the ways in which a profession is historically and socially constructed. It considers the significance of processes of occupational closure and the role of the professional association in organizing, creating, and defining professional behaviour and practices. The chapter concludes by discussing the research methods used in this study.

Chapter 2 explores the role of education in the professional project. It links the development of public relations university education with the massification of Australian higher education in the 1970s and 1980s, and identifies challenges for public relations in the academy. Drawing on archives and interviews, the chapter investigates the early interest of professional institutes in regulating the education and training of practitioners and the introduction of an accreditation programme for university courses in 1991. The findings reveal resistance to scholarly learning among some senior practitioners as PRIA sought an increasing role in university education and a stronger alignment with business faculties in the 1990s.

Chapter 3 investigates the significance of gender for public relations in the last century and the changing relationship between women and public relations. Although public relations offered opportunities for individual—albeit primarily middle-class women—throughout the twentieth century, and women played a role in the post-war development of public relations, the gender composition of the public relations workforce began to change significantly in the 1970s. This chapter argues the overall increase in women working in public relations resulted in a gendered stratification of public relations work. The marginalization of certain activity also constrained the construction of public relations knowledge and expertise partly in response to growing concern in the 1980s and 1990s that a feminized workforce would devalue public relations and, threaten its attempts to gain professional recognition.

Chapter 4 considers the significance of globalization in the second half of the twentieth century and the impact of transnational activity and colonial networks on Australian public relations. Archival research reveals the Australian institutes' strong focus on the British public relations industry in the 1950s and suggests the US industry was not necessarily the "catalyst" that mainstream and conventional histories suggest. In addition, the Australian industry was increasingly involved in Asia, developing the careers of individual practitioners and encouraging the expansion of Australian consultancies. This chapter investigates the significance of transnational activity for the development of an Australian professional occupational identity.

Finally, the conclusion draws links between the historical development of public relations in Australia and globally and the ways in which public relations knowledge and expertise were conceptualized and contested. It identifies the significance of these findings for contemporary understandings of public relations.

Kate Fitch
Murdoch University
Perth, Australia

CHAPTER 1

The Professionalization of Public Relations

Abstract Histories of public relations tend to focus on its evolutionary development to the modern profession. This chapter considers professionalization, that is, the processes by which practitioners and professional associations seek to establish public relations as a unique service over which they hold a monopoly. Using historical narratives of Australian public relations, it identifies competing ideologies and tensions in constructing a public relations body of knowledge and the implications for historical understandings of the development of public relations. This chapter highlights historiographical challenges in writing public relations history. It concludes by outlining the research methods used in this study, which included the analysis of archival research and semi-structured interviews.

Keywords Australia • History • Historiography • Professional associations • Professionalization • Public relations

INTRODUCTION

The focus of this chapter is professionalization, drawing on recent scholarship on public relations historiography and sociological writing on the professions. It argues there is a significant gap in the public relations literature in terms of how public relations associations attempt to develop

© The Editor(s) (if applicable) and The Author(s) 2016   1
K. Fitch, *Professionalizing Public Relations*,
DOI 10.1057/978-1-137-57309-4_1

professional legitimacy, despite the field's preoccupation with its professional status. This preoccupation has led to normative histories, which frame public relations history as an evolutionary and linear development towards an ethical profession. More critical histories reveal the links with broader societal shifts and allow the "development" of public relations to be understood in terms of increasing occupational closure. This chapter concludes with a brief discussion of the methods used in this research.

PROFESSIONALIZATION, INSTITUTIONALIZATION, AND EDUCATION

Understanding Professionalization

Until the early 1970s, professions were understood as a moral force and a stabilizing influence on society, or were described primarily in terms of their socially functional traits, such as altruism, or through the characteristics which distinguished them from occupations (Davis, 2005; Macdonald, 1995). However, sociologists began to focus on "the unusually effective, monopolistic institutions of professions and their high status as the critical factor and treated knowledge, skill, and ethical orientations not as objective characteristics but rather as ideology" (Freidson, 1986, p. 29). For example, Everett C. Hughes reframed the investigation of the professions in 1963, but the significance was not recognized until much later: "what are the circumstances in which people in an occupation attempt to turn it into a profession and themselves into professional people?" (Hughes, 1963, as cited in Macdonald, 1995, p. 6). This book investigates professionalization, that is, "the process by which producers of special services sought to constitute *and control* a market for their expertise" and recognizes that such expertise is "founded on a system of education and credentialing" (Larson, 1977, p. xvi, xvii). Viewing the profession as a historical construct, rather than a static entity whose characteristics could be catalogued and described, allowed sociologists to focus on the development of an occupation to a profession (Pieczka & L'Etang, 2006).

Contemporary research into the sociology of professions therefore focuses on issues of occupational closure, social stratification, social exclusion, state formation, and the development of a capitalist economic order (Muzio & Kirkpatrick, 2011). In addition, Muzio and Kirkpatrick (2011) call for a greater focus on organizations, noting professional activity takes place largely in organizational settings and in academic institutions.

Professional projects are institutionalization projects that advance by claiming intellectual and economic space in competition with other professions (Abbott, 1988; Suddaby & Viale, 2011). However, liberal organizational professions, of which public relations is one example, struggle "to realize the degree of indetermination, monopolization, and control of their knowledge base … their professional project is closely related to attempts to harness, colonize and monopolize organizational spaces, processes, and policies" (Reed, 1996, p. 584, 585). This brief review of ideas about the profession confirms that it is a construct of a particular social and historical context.

The Role of Professional Associations

Professions are processes of occupational closure that marshal exclusionary and demarcatory strategies to control access, regulate professional practice, and institutionalize those practices (Davies, 1996; Noordegraaf, 2011; Witz, 1992). Professional associations play a pivotal role in organizing, creating, and defining professional behaviour and practices, and in doing so, asserting occupational closure (Noordegraaf, 2011), and are therefore are an important "springboard…that enabled PR to develop into a distinct field" (Watson, 2015, p. 6). The first public relations professional associations emerged after the World War II. The Public Relations Society of America (PRSA) was founded in 1947, and emerged out of two established councils. The UK-Based Institute of Public Relations (IPR) was founded in 1948 (it became the CIPR when it gained chartered status in 2005). The following decades saw professional associations established throughout the world, including Public Relations Institute of South Africa in 1957; Argentinian Public Relations Association in 1958; Institute of Public Relations Malaysia in 1965; Institute of Public Relations Singapore (IPRS) in 1970; Public Relations Association of Trinidad and Tobago in 1972; Public Relations Association of Uganda in 1975; and China Public Relations Association in 1987. The International Public Relations Association (IPRA) was established in 1955, following earlier discussions by two Dutch and four British practitioners dating back to 1949 (International P.R. Association, 1955; L'Etang, 2004; Watson & Macnamara, 2013).

In Australia, various public relations institutes were established from 1950 but were primarily state based.[1] The Australian Institute of Public Relations (AIPR) was established in Sydney in 1950; Public Relations

Institute of Australia (Victoria) (PRIA [Vic]) was founded in 1952; and the South Australian chapter in 1956 (Gleeson, 2014; Sheehan, 2014a); the Tasmanian institute was incorporated and officially affiliated with the national council in 1967 (Tasmania at Last, 1967); and a Western Australian institute was not established until late 1970 (New W.A. Chapter, 1971). A loose association of state institutes was only formed in 1960, and a national organization was not established until 1994; until then, state institutes tended to operate independently (Gleeson, 2014). Newsletters produced by "the public relations institutes of Australia" sometimes represented only the states of New South Wales (NSW) and Victoria. However, these PRIA forerunners were not the only professional associations interested in public relations; for example, Australian Association of Advertising Agencies (4As), established in 1946, saw public relations as their domain (Sinclair, 2014, p. 6), and the Victorian Institute of Public Affairs promoted public relations as valuable in promoting employee relations and developing organizational narratives and that "the only worthwhile public relations activities, however, are those based on 'good performance—publicly appreciated'" (Wide Scope, 1951). Even in the 1960s, some practitioners argued that public relations people should be members of the Australian Journalists Association (AJA) (To The Editor, 1966). Individual practitioners maintained membership of international organizations; for example, AIPR councillors E Colin Davis and Asher Joel were PRSA members and PRIA (Vic) members sought affiliation with IPR and became overseas members of the British institute (What We're Doing, 1955).

The Australian public relations institutes were often not the only institute to which members belonged. In addition to being a Fellow and the foundation president of both PRIA (Vic) and PRIA, the professional memberships of Noel Griffiths, who worked in the banking sector from the 1930s until his retirement in 1965, included: Fellow of the Advertising Institute of Australia, Chartered Institute of Secretaries, and Bankers' Institute of Australia; Associate Fellow of the Australian Institute of Management; and Associate of the Australian Society of Accountants (Profile: Noel Griffiths, 1965; Stanger, 1966). Griffiths was also the President of the Advertising Institute of Australia 1962–1963, and served two terms on the IPRA Council between 1960 and 1962 (Watson & Macnamara, 2013). Asher Joel, a founding member of AIPR and its third president, belonged to so many organizations, boards, and committees that his friends "would refer to him as a great 'Joiner'" (Thomson, 1956, p. 4). In addition to being an AIPR Fellow, his professional affiliations included Fellow of

Royal Commonwealth Society; Fellow of Royal Society of Arts; Fellow of the Advertising Institute of Australia; Fellow of the Australian Institute of Management; and membership of the AJA and PRSA (Parliament of NSW, n.d.; Thomson, 1956).

Noordegraaf identifies three mechanisms used by professional associations seeking professional status:

- *Cognitive mechanisms*: schooling, education, training, knowledge, skills, conferences, books, journals, and magazines;
- *Normative mechanisms*: membership criteria, selection criteria, entry barriers, certificates, codes of conducts, sanctions, and discipline;
- *Symbolic mechanisms*: rites of passage, stories, heroes, codes of ethics, service ideals, and missions. (2011, p. 470)

These mechanisms jointly "define work practices, demarcate occupational fields, regulate behaviours, symbolize professionalism and provide external cues" (Noordegraaf, 2011, p. 470). For example, a journal produced by a professional association and read by the practitioner body is significant for "the disciplining effect of its coverage is to contribute to the construction of a relatively coordinated and consistent understanding across the field of what PR is, where it belongs, and how it should be practised" (Edwards & Pieczka, 2013, p. 20). It is not difficult to relate these mechanisms to the activities of professional public relations institutes over several decades. For example, cognitive mechanisms include PRIA-endorsed books, *The Australian Public Relations Handbook* (Dwyer, 1961) and *Public Relations Practice in Australia* (Potts, 1976), with chapters written primarily by senior PRIA members; the production of state and national newsletters, including *Pro-Files* (1952–1958), *P.R. News* [c. 1954–1956], *Public Relations Journal*, renamed *Public Relations Australia* in 1968 [1965–1972], *Profile* [c. 1983–2002], *Public Relations* [c. 1990–2001], *The PRofessional* [ca. 1996]; the establishment of national conferences; the introduction of education and training courses; and the development of accreditation criteria for university courses in 1991. Normative mechanisms include the introduction of new membership criteria and entry barriers in 1986, including the need for professional-grade members to hold an the development of accredited degree or pass a written examination. Symbolic mechanisms include the introduction of new ethics codes for PRIA and the creation in 1987 of the College of Fellows, in that the Fellows, as an elite, invitation-only membership category represent senior expertise and professional knowledge, and are responsible for the ethical regulation of the industry. In addition, practitioner perspectives offer both "rites of passage" and even heroes; Asher Joel, for instance, is described as "the Australian public relations pioneer" (Sheehan, 2007, p. 5), "Australia's First PR Knight" (1971), and received the industry's "Man of Achievement" award for "outstanding achievements in the community interest in the field of public relations" in 1970 (NSW's Man of Achievement, 1970). In the same vein, Morath's (2008) book of interviews with senior PRIA members is subtitled: "Conversations with Australia's Public Relations Legends". Noordegraaf (2011) notes the successful institutionalization of these mechanisms strengthens claims for professional status by helping to ensure occupational closure. This closure is established by professional associations through both formal and informal credentialism (Edwards, 2014).

Professionalization and Education

Education plays a key role in processes of professionalization (Faulconbridge & Muzio, 2009; Noordegraaf, 2011), by legitimizing a field, defining its body of knowledge, and offering qualifications that can be used for occupational closure (L'Etang, 1999, 2008a). Education therefore can be used to justify a field's monopoly on a set of occupational practices. Universities are key actors in professionalization, and, from the industry perspective, the regulation of education and training is important in ensuring quality and competency in future practitioners (Faulconbridge & Muzio, 2009). However, there is little information on the dynamic between universities and practitioners in terms of how this professionalization occurs (de Bussy & Wolf, 2009; Faulconbridge & Muzio, 2009).

Investigating industry attempts to regulate university education can therefore offer important insights into how a professional association both constitutes public relations knowledge and understands education as an important mechanism of professionalization (Faulconbridge & Muzio, 2009; Noordegraaf, 2011). The role of university education in professionalization will be investigated in Chapter 2. However, it is worth acknowledging that public relations has suffered weak institutionalization in the Australian academy due in part to its close industry links, its vocational orientation, and threats of encroachment from other fields, such as marketing, advertising, and even journalism, despite the industry's attempts to establish its unique disciplinary status (Fitch, 2013; McKie & Hunt, 1999; Hatherell & Bartlett, 2006). Researching how the public relations industry sought to claim professional status, through the application of specialized knowledge for social and economic gain (Larson, 1977) and, in turn, the constitution and institutionalization of that knowledge, is significant in that such research allows an understanding of how power is manifest through particular institutional structures and professionalizing processes.

Education plays a significant role in the transmission and reproduction of knowledge and was the site of contest between conflicting perspectives on public relations knowledge. Its increasing institutionalization in the academy led to widespread concern about the value of tertiary education. A panel of directors of "Australia's leading public relations agencies" at a recent Australian industry conference lamented the poor training of university graduates, arguing "agencies are at the coal face and are seeing what is happening a lot more quickly" than universities (Christensen, 2014). The "failure" of public relations education is a persistent trope. This elevation of practical or professional expertise is significant for public relations, where many practitioners perceive a schism between theory and practice and tend to value practical expertise over abstract knowledge (Byrne, 2008; van Ruler, 2005), with implications for the industry regulation of public relations education. In a number of studies, critical scholars explore the role of knowledge in the constitution of public relations as a profession, that is, the ways in which "a body of practical knowledge" rather than abstract knowledge is constructed and indeed valued in the industry (Pieczka, 2006, p. 281). These studies include participant observation of senior British practitioners on a training course and analysis of campaign entries for the annual IPR awards in the UK (Pieczka, 2000, 2002, 2006, 2007); histories of British public relations and public relations education (L'Etang, 1999, 2004); and analysis of the professional narratives of three public relations associations, including PRIA (Breit & Demetrious, 2010). They argue public relations has a weak ethical culture and a thin body of knowledge and expertise (Breit & Demetrious, 2010), and that public relations expertise is constructed by practitioners as "constituted and transmitted through practice" (Pieczka, 2002, p. 321).

AUSTRALIAN PUBLIC RELATIONS HISTORIES

Textbook Histories and Practitioner Perspectives

The history of public relations in Australia has largely been defined through information in textbooks (see, for example, Harrison, 2011; Potts, 1976; Quarles & Rowlings, 1993; Tymson, Lazar, & Lazar, 2008;

Zawawi, 2009); in practitioner memoirs and speeches (see Flower J., 2007; Potts, 2008; Turnbull, 2010); or published interviews, profiles, and even obituaries of "pioneer" practitioners (see Morath, 2008; Nicholls, 2007; PRIA, 2010; Sheehan, 2010). As such, the practitioner perspective—noting nearly all twentieth-century Australian public relations textbooks were written by practitioners—dominates. In fact, there is a dearth of both scholarly histories and documentary evidence regarding the recent history of Australian public relations; Turner, for instance, notes "the sparse documentation of the growth of PR in the period from the 1970s through the 1990s" (2002, p. 223), and Sheehan (2007) similarly points to the "paucity" of historical records. The industry's history in Australia is primarily a history of PRIA and prominent PRIA members, and their attempts to claim professional recognition for public relations. In these textbook histories, public relations in Australia is considered to date from the arrival of General Douglas MacArthur and his public relations staff in 1943; one staff member, Asher Joel, set up a public relations consultancy after the war and helped establish the professional association (Zawawi, 2009). Typically, authors describe World War II as "a catalyst for PR development" (Harrison, 2011, p. 65); "the catalyst to allow public relations to develop into a fully fledged profession" (Zawawi, 2009, p. 44); or describe how the Australian public relations industry "took off" in the war and the following decade (Flower J., 2007, p. 179). Since, then, public relations is perceived to have evolved significantly and "in its current form is a modern profession" (Harrison, 2011, p. 39). Public relations history is thus a record of high-profile contributors who shaped the field in the post-war years; the "history" section on PRIA's website (see http://www.pria.com.au/aboutus/history-) offers links to biographies for Fellows, the senior, prestigious, invitation-only membership category; past presidents; and "in honour" (that is, obituaries for prominent figures associated with the professional association, including, among others, Joel). Thus, historical understandings of public relations are considered primarily in terms of the activities and achievements of individual PRIA members and the establishment of the professional association.

Writing the history of a field that is arguably struggling for professional recognition and social legitimacy can be fraught. As L'Etang (2008b) warns, such histories can too easily become a justification and legitimation of the field. Textbooks written by practitioners, rather than scholars, result in a history that presents uncritically a narrative of evolution and progress (Hoy, Raaz, & Weimara, 2007). To offer one example, Australian textbook histories attribute tertiary-level education and industry accreditation of university courses to confirmation of the field's professional status (see, for example, Zawawi, 2009) and ignore the broader societal changes, such as the massification and marketization of Australian higher education, that allowed public relations to become established as a course of study (Fitch, 2014b). There is therefore a need to examine the processes and values underpinning widely accepted narratives, which position Australian public relations in terms of evolutionary growth towards professional standing and ethical practice. A few scholars have begun to call for Australian public relations history to be reconceptualized, arguing it is incorrect to attribute the origin of public relations to war-time public information campaigns and the post-war period and identifying a number of Australian campaigns prior to World War II (Crawford & Macnamara, 2012; Macnamara & Crawford, 2010; Sheehan, 2007). These scholars suggest these approaches are based on a narrow understanding of public relations and argue textbook authors have focused primarily on public relations consultants and ignored other public relations activity (Sheehan, 2007) or relied uncritically on "the subjective perspective of PR practitioners" (Crawford & Macnamara, 2012, p. 45). I argue that standard historical narratives of public relations in Australia have therefore led to an uncritical and unproblematic understanding of its development.

Public Relations in the Mid-twentieth Century

Rather than a linear progression towards a modern profession, this book approaches the historical development of public relations in Australia in terms of a competitive jostling with other co-emergent fields. It therefore focuses on the dynamic and at times contradictory understandings of public relations, that is, shifts in meaning and overlaps with other occupational practices. Public relations existed prior to World War II, but it was beginning to gain recognition as a distinct occupation, albeit closely related to and considerably overlapping with advertising, marketing, and other promotional work. Crawford and Macnamara identify the "nomenclature of practices" around public relations activity, and particularly the slippage or shifts between advertising, publicity, and public relations as "a central historiographical issue" (2014, p. 273). For example, in the first decade of professional associations, the 1950s, public relations was conceived broadly as any form of public engagement, and ranged from window displays and press relations to radio and film production. Much public relations work was conducted by advertising agencies, although this information is excluded from most conventional histories of public relations and advertising in Australia.

Given the significance of interprofessional competition for the development of a professional occupational identity (Abbott, 1988), it is revealing to consider both how the emergent public relations industry related to and attempted to distinguish itself from fields such as journalism, advertising, marketing, and other media and communication industries by claiming a particular and unique field of expertise. In the mid-twentieth century, it is at times difficult to see how such occupations were distinguished. For example, in his history of Australian advertising, Crawford (2008) cites Goldberg, who ran one of three advertising agencies appointed by the War Effort Publicity Board (WEPB) to manage press advertising, radio advertising, and specialized media on the importance of advertising for the war effort: "Advertising today is part of a wide-spreading propaganda machine concerned with the all-important task of *moulding public opinion*" (cited in Crawford, 2008, p. 107). Even after the war, when WEPB became the Australian Advertising Council, agencies produced government propaganda films (Crawford, 2008; Sinclair, 2014). Further, it was increasingly difficult to distinguish between "propaganda, advertising and entertainment" (Crawford, 2008, p. 108). For example, radio programmes were a key promotional tool with Colgate-Palmolive sponsoring George Patterson's production of variety radio programmes (Crawford, 2008, p. 110) and the conservative Australian Liberal Party's public relations strategy for the 1949 election included the radio programme, John Henry Austral, and quizzes, developed by the Hansen-Rubensohn advertising agency (Griffen-Foley, 2002, 2003). Ward (1999) maintains the Liberal Party's use of radio was copied from US and Canadian political campaigns dating from before World War II. Of relevance is the ongoing involvement of members of public relations state institutes in the 1950s in both advertising agencies and radio production.

Indeed, many members of the newly formed professional institutes for public relations worked across advertising, marketing, and public relations, in radio and film production, or had a background in journalism (Fitch, 2016). Retrospective accounts of the work history of public relations "experts" are offered in the short biographies of contributors to Dwyer's (1961) *The Australian Public Relations Handbook* and speakers at the first national public relations convention in 1966. Esta Handfield, later the first female president of PRIA (Vic), came to public relations through radio and advertising; her first public relations role was with the Department of Post-War Reconstruction (The Speakers, 1966). George Stapleton, another PRIA (Vic) president and owner of Pegasus Public Relations, "supervised, scripted, or directed over 30 documentary films" working in public relations roles in the oil industry over a 24-year period (Dwyer, 1961, p. 132). PRIA (Vic) member, Geoff Waye, entered public relations in 1950 after a career in journalism; in 1960, he worked as a copy director for a Melbourne-based advertising and marketing consultancy (Dwyer, 1961, p. 200). Graham Lomas, who was a public relations officer with the British Army during the war, described his "lifetime in advertising, journalism and public relations activities" (Dwyer, 1961, p. 220). These accounts of public relations careers are typical.

One account of a public relations department before and after World War II reveals useful insights into understandings of the development of public relations as a unique field of expertise. Retrospectivity in Australian practitioner accounts is significant in that such narratives are structured within a dominant paradigm that promotes an evolutionary professional development for public relations (Fitch, 2015). In 1956, PRIA (Vic)'s immediate past president E. Bennet Bremner had just established himself as a consultant, but he retained Qantas as a client, as he had run their public relations division (Sparrow, 1956). Bremner described his work for Qantas publicity before the war when "in 1938 [it] covered the whole of the field of advertising, publicity and public relations" and after the war when "in 1950, he organised the breaking up of the department into advertising and P.R. divisions, assuming the title of Chief Press and P.R. Officer" (Meet the Members, 1956). This account by the former president frames the professional development of public relations as a growing separation between public relations and advertising functions.

Professional Dilemmas in the 1960s and 1970s

The *Public Relations Journal*, renamed *Public Relations Australia* from 1968, was produced by PRIA from 1965 to 1972. It was billed as the "journal of the Public Relations Institutes of Australia," but in 1967, the journal represented only the state-based institutes of NSW, Victoria, South Australia, and Queensland. The Tasmanian institute contributed from 1968, and the Western Australian institute contributed from early 1971.

However, members across Australia were identified in specific issues prior to the establishment of formal state institutes in Tasmania and Western Australia.

Public relations is presented in the Australian journal as primarily press relations, publications (such as annual reports and brochures), and community engagement (through various activities, including documentary films). A substantial government report into public relations in the public sector in Victoria and NSW confirms these findings in that it identifies public relations activity as press relations, press cuttings, publicity, publications, displays and exhibitions, opening ceremonies, and, in some cases, printing and photography (Hutchinson, 1970). Kaldor, whose academic research on public relations was summarized in a four-page report in the journal, characterized the majority of Australian practitioners as ex-journalists and public relations work as typically press relations, product publicity, editing, writing, and general promotional work, and contrasted "the realities of PR practice" with the rhetoric around professionalism and management (1967, p. 5). Whereas in previous decades, a wide variety of experience could lead into public relations work, job advertisements in the journal in the late 1960s and early 1970s refer to "considerable journalistic experience" as the primary qualification (see, for example, Hydro-electric commission, 1968).

Themes around the professional standing of public relations are prominent, with an emphasis on university education, profiles of senior (male) members, membership upgrades, and professional development. Articles report industry events and news, including new appointments, elections to state and national councils, luncheons, conferences, book and film reviews, case studies, and include features about aspects of industry practice, lecture tours by visiting academics, or profiles of senior practitioners. The granting of permission for PRIA members in Western Australia to practise in West Perth, where only "professionals" were allowed to work, was reported as a victory (Victory in W.A., 1967). Given that professionalism necessarily demands claiming a unique domain of expertise (Abbott, 1988), it is significant Kaldor argues, "the eclectic techniques utilised in PR practice are not distinctly separable from such as fields as marketing, advertising, printing and journalism" (1967, p. 5), and that the majority of practitioners are ex-journalists. Less than half, that is, 45% or 83 of the 176 public relations companies listed in Australian capital city directories had PRIA members (Kaldor, 1967) suggesting that the professional association struggled to attract people who identified as public relations practitioners as members.

The Expansion of Public Relations in the 1980s

In the 1980s, the Australian public relations industry grew significantly. Its domain expanded from primarily media relations and promotion to serving the expanding corporate sector with new functions such as investor relations and public affairs (Fitch & Third, 2010). Turner, Bonner, and Marshall (2000) and Turnbull (2010) argue the mid-1980s saw a significant growth in the consultancy sector in Australia, peaking in 1986. The number of consultancies increased more than four-fold in a ten-year period, from 58 or 59 agencies in 1976 to 270 in 1986.[2] This growth in the consultancy sector is significant in terms of the professionalization of public relations and the demarcation of the field as a unique area of expertise (L'Etang, 2004). In the 1980s and 1990s, public relations also became more institutionalized in the Australian government sector, with the appointment of ministerial media advisors and the establishment of media units and public affairs teams (Butler, 1998; Ward, 2003). In tandem, the growth in communication professions in Australia increased employment opportunities, fuelling the growth in public relations education (Putnis, 1993). The economic downturn associated with the global financial crisis in October 1987 contributed to a significant restructuring of the public relations and advertising industries in Australia (Crawford, 2008; Turnbull, 2010).

Concerns over public relations' poor image and legitimacy and professional standing are illustrated in newspaper articles, trade publications, and industry newsletters throughout the 1980s. A PRIA-commissioned report acknowledged the challenges associated with the changing industry profile, given the industry's rapid growth and the increase in tertiary qualifications among practitioners (PR Industry, 1985). However, the report identified low salary levels in comparison with other business functions and a significant variance in salaries between male and female participants, with 23% of male participants and 66% of female study participants earning less than $30,000 per annum. Public relations practitioners are described in one newspaper feature in the early 1980s as "the used car salesmen of the communications world: useful but suspect" and "the image of PR remains a kind of fast-talking hocus-pocus, a sort of witchery little understood by those outside the industry" (Dell'oso, 1983, p. 29). This article offers the standard historical narrative, attributing the origin of public relations to Ivy Lee in the USA at the turn of the century and citing the origins of Australian public relations as emerging in the late 1940s. The journalist draws on interviews with David Potts (who was interviewed for the research reported in this book), then senior lecturer in communication at Mitchell College of Advanced Education, and Tony Benner, PRIA president, to suggest that public relations had changed from the "used car salesman" analogy. Both maintain public relations is now "respectable" and that PRIA is "having a clear-up campaign ... The PR 'as fast-talking charlatan' is an image we are trying to get rid of" (Benner, as cited in Dell'oso, 1983, p. 29). Indeed, as PRIA state president Bill Mackey (who later served a term as national president and was also interviewed for this research) reported in a Western Australian industry newsletter in 1984, the national council aimed to "strengthen" the institute and "to give members a greater sense of belonging to a national association" (Major Plans, 1984). These aims were to be achieved through research into the industry, the appointment of a national director and office, the establishment of a public relations research and education foundation and a Board of Fellows, and reviews of membership grades, professional accreditation, and the Code of Ethics. The PRIA national council therefore introduced a number of strategies in the mid- to late 1980s with the express aim of establishing public relations' professional standing. The new membership criteria required either a practitioner examination or an approved university degree to be eligible for professional-grade membership. These strategies were not universally popular (WA State Council, 1985). The first practitioner accreditation examination was offered in 1986, and only practitioners with at least five-years experience were eligible (Candidates Sought, 1986; First PR Accreditation, 1986). In fact, the practitioner examination was not popular with senior practitioners.[3] In response, the PRIA national council agreed late in 1989 to introduce an oral examination, later referred to as a senior professional assessment, for practitioners with at least ten years' experience (Oral Examination, 1990). PRIA founded the College of Fellows in 1987 to recognize the achievements of senior members (many of whom did not meet the newly introduced criteria for PRIA membership).[4] Fellow membership was invitation only. These strategies, and indeed, the professional standing of public relations, are the focus of various articles in two lift-out feature sections in the influential, business-orientated newspaper, *Australian Financial Review,* in 1986 and 1988. The articles are written by high-profile PRIA members rather than journalists, and the lift-outs are presumably funded through industry advertising. These practitioner-written articles are revealing in the way authors position public relations within a professional framework. One author distances "professional" public relations from "flim flam" and "razzamattaz," asserting the need for "sound research" (Jabara, 1986, p. 52). Tom Flower, who managed Eric White Associates (EWA) offices in Sydney, Hong King, and Singapore in the 1960s, advises on the selection of a public relations consultancy:

> How do you distinguish the true professionals from the mediocre or worse found in every professional group? ... Ask whether the principal and senior staff of the consultancy are members of the Public Relations Institute of Australia (PRIA). Since 1986, new membership or associateship has been available only to those who pass accreditation exams, or to graduates of recognised tertiary communication courses who have served a work experience requirement. (1988, p. 64)

T. Flower refers to another professional association, the Society of Business Communicators, acknowledging their commitment to improving practical communication skills but suggesting "good public relations is much broader and involves counselling at the highest level" (1988, p. 64); it is clear PRIA seeks to establish its domain over the latter. Emerging from this distinction is a clear bifurcation between "practical" and technical communication skills and strategy and high-level "counselling" of business leaders. In one article titled *Professionalism Heralds New Era*, the PRIA president makes grand claims for the international standing of Australian public relations, arguing Australia "has a higher standard of people, better and more effective ideas and techniques" than the USA and the UK (MacIntosh, 1986, p. 45). He points to the introduction of "accreditation by examination for those practitioners not holding recognised tertiary degrees" as an important PRIA initiative in "improving industry standards" and "the industry image" (MacIntosh, p. 45).

Perceptions of the role played by education are significant. The outgoing national president, B. Mackey, in an industry newsletter article titled *Looking Back on a Dramatic Decade*, described "the explosion in tertiary education in public relations" as a "triumph" (1989, p. 3). Jim Pritchett, managing director of Shandwick Australia and future IPRA president, noted the changing demographics of the industry with the growth in communication graduates: "consultancies are being run by people who have communication degrees … [and] who will lead the profession into the next century" (1988, p. 62). An article by Potts, who played a major role in the development of public relations education and the regulation of professional structures, tells what is now the standard and widely accepted narrative of public relations education in Australia: that it started in the early 1970s, with courses at Mitchell College of Advanced Education in Bathurst, NSW, and at Queensland Institute of Technology (QIT) in Brisbane, Queensland, and that such courses reflect "the growing sophistication in the public relations industry in that its practitioners are coming more out of formal courses of study in public relations and less out of journalism" (Potts, 1986, p. 50). In addition, Potts writes "PRIA, in an effort to raise further the quality of PR performance, has also … introduced a requirement that for full membership of the institute one must now have a degree or pass an institute-set examination" (1986, p. 50). Education is perceived by PRIA at this time to play a pivotal role in raising industry standards and in regulating membership of the institute. As such, the historical newspaper articles referred to in this section place public relations education firmly within a professional discourse. The significance of education for the professional project is discussed in Chapter 2.

Restructuring Public Relations in the 1990s

PRIA was primarily a state-based organization in that its members belonged to the state-based institutes rather than the national body. In November 1990, the PRIA president noted "the current federated system is a hindrance to achieving the objectives of the Institute for both a professional and a financial perspective" (Ray, 1990; see also National Journal, 1990). There was considerable tension between some states and the national organization, even after formal incorporation of the national body in 1994, particularly as NSW and Victorian institutes had the largest membership, and the national office was run out of NSW. For example, many states refused to pay a requested A$10 levy per member to support a national newsletter, and NSW and Victorian institutes combined to produce a newsletter for their members following the collapse of the national newsletter (Anderson, 1990). In fact, discussions regarding the need for a single national institute were evident from the early years of state institutes in the 1950s.

In 1996, the PRIA (NSW) council surveyed its membership by sector and found the majority of its members worked in the consultancy sector (41.2%) and the corporate sector (32.6%); only a small percentage worked in government (6.2%) and not-for-profit sectors (4.8%) (Corporates on the Way Up, 1996). In response to these statistics, the state council developed a campaign to recruit more practitioners from the corporate sector, concerned that they were underrepresented in their membership profile despite already comprising the second largest membership group. Given the growth in public relations roles within government identified earlier in this chapter, it is perhaps surprising that the government sector was not the focus of this campaign, which suggests the Australian professional association sought to align public relations primarily with the corporate sector. L'Etang (2004) noted in the UK that government public relations activity had never been subject to the same professionalization agenda.

Many PRIA activities in this decade were focused on jurisdictional issues and the regulation of public relations activity. For example, the PRIA national board and state committees were concerned with possible encroachment from rival fields such as journalism and marketing.[5] There are concerns expressed in board minutes and newsletter articles about AJA (and its subsequent incarnation, Media Entertainment and Arts Alliance) seeking to represent public relations practitioners and to ensure practitioners' wages and working conditions are covered by an award, and even to accredit university public relations courses (AJA Log of Claims, 1992; AJA Interference, 1993). Another organization, the Australian Institute of Professional Communicators planned to accredit courses and award scholarships (Starck, 1999). In 1994, Marjorie Anderson, chair of PRIA's National Education Committee (NEC), represented PRIA at the newly formed Council of Australian Marketing Service Associations (CAMSA), of which PRIA was a founding member. The PRIA national council endorsed a preferred definition of CAMSA member organizations as "marketing and communication-related organisations" rather than "marketing-communication-related organisations"; that is, the board was adamant that public relations was not a sub-set of marketing but a distinct field of expertise.[6] Turnbull (2010) maintains the Australian Centre for Corporate Public Affairs, founded in 1990, was an influential network for senior public relations practitioners working in big business and the corporate sphere. PRIA attempted to define and indeed promote its understanding of professional public relations to show how it differed, for instance, from the concerns of the Society of Business Communicators and the Australian Centre for Corporate Public Affairs, and to distinguish its members as professionals able to offer high-level business strategy and counselling. Interestingly, Turnbull, a PRIA Fellow, states that PRIA "has become less and less relevant to the industry," primarily because of its "early founder obsession with declaring public relations a 'profession'"; its failure to attract a representative membership; and its subsequent "status anxiety" (2010, p. 28).

Research Methods

The research reported in this book emerged from my interest in investigating how particular understandings of public relations and public relations education in Australia became widely accepted. I recognize that as a researcher, I am not a neutral instrument but part of the meaning-making that occurs through data collection, analysis, and interpretation and in the construction of an historical narrative. I therefore acknowledge my subjectivity by identifying my involvement with the field under study. I have taught public relations in a university since 2001, and prior to that worked in public relations roles in arts, community, and government sectors. The significance for the research reported in this book is that building on this practitioner experience, I have worked as a public relations educator and scholar for more than 15 years and reflected on the challenges of teaching and researching public relations in a dynamic higher education environment.

I acknowledge my ongoing association with, and membership of, PRIA. I developed a public relations course in 2006 that was subsequently accredited by the professional association. I played an active role in PRIA (Western Australia [WA])'s state council (2005–2008) and the National Education Committee (NEC) (2008–2011). PRIA and NEC membership possibly facilitated access to participants in this study in that they perceived I was part of their professional network. In addition, these links may have facilitated access to PRIA archives, although locating and gaining access to PRIA archives was not straightforward.

I collected evidence through archival research and interviews. I drew on national and state-based professional institute archives for the research reported in this book, consulting newsletters produced by state and national councils and that are available in the State Library of New South Wales and the State Library of Victoria; the PRIA (National) and PRIA (NSW) board minutes that are archived in the Mitchell Library; and other reports, booklets, promotional material, and documents that are archived in these libraries and in the Battye Library in the State Library of Western Australia. In addition, I consulted two privately held collections of PRIA records: the records of the chair of PRIA's NEC throughout the 1990s, which I have previously referred as the Anderson Archives (Fitch, 2014a)[7]; and the PRIA (WA) state council records, which in 2013 were stored privately in the home of the state council's administrative officer. I also drew on digitized newspaper records across Australia.

Between December 2010 and September 2012, I interviewed 14 practitioners and educators who were involved in Australian public relations from the 1970s through to 2000. I interviewed equal numbers of men and women, seeking participants who had prominent roles in the industry or in education. The first participant self-selected and subsequent participants were recruited via snowball sampling or identified through archival research. I include an interview schedule (see Appendix A) recording interview dates, participant names (where participants chose to be identified), and PRIA membership status.[8] Participants represent a diverse range of experiences (Fitch, 2014b). As I have argued elsewhere, the retrospective accounts offered by key informants were shaped by their contemporary perspectives on public relations, its development and what they perceived as their role in that development (Fitch, 2015).

I adopt a constructivist approach in that I do not believe historical sources, be they archives or interviews with participants in historical events, offer "direct, unmediated and uncomplicated access to the past" (Thomson, 2012, p. 102). Constructivist approaches question how social realities are produced (Holstein & Gubrium, 2008), and therefore suit my interest in investigating how particular understandings of public relations in Australia became widely accepted. This epistemological orientation influenced the research design. For example, the recognition of archives, and indeed of archivization, as historical processes subject to political concerns and as sites of contested meaning is relevant for this research in that it identifies how these processes inform the knowledge that is produced and constituted (Steedman, 2002; King, 2012). Both issues of access, including geographical distance, and the incompleteness of professional institute records influenced the design, focus, and findings of the research reported in this book, and are significant challenges to the construction of an historical narrative.

Interviews can usefully address the limitations of archival research, including gaps in the archives and the lack of documentation of (particularly, informal) processes and discussions that contribute to decisions (Tansey, 2007). But interviews, like archives, do not offer neutral information (Fontana & Frey, 2000). As I established earlier in this chapter, contemporary understandings of the development of Australian public relations rely heavily on the subjective experiences of practitioners. Given the lack of alternate evidence, retrospective accounts, such as those narrated in memoirs and interviews, have become the de facto history of public relations. There are profound methodological implications of the uncritical use of personal testimony and retrospective narratives, and in particular of the subjective experiences of senior practitioners, for the constitution of public relations history in that such accounts tend to offer narrow understandings of public relations within a dominant narrative of professionalization (Fitch, 2015). The perceptions reported by participants in my research reinforce the need for a critical approach, particularly in relation to "eyewitness" accounts, and for scholars to interrogate the constitution of public relations history. The ways in which high-profile participants whose perspectives were mediated by their professional success and their elite status within the professional association remember and reconstruct their memories and perceptions offer evidence of the discourses, which informed—and, I argue, continue to inform—public relations in Australia. That is, their retrospective accounts are framed within contemporary understandings of the field and its development and their role in the professional project.

I analysed archives and interviews, identifying themes that broadly relate to the relationship between education, gender, and professionalization and the constitution of public relations knowledge. I combined analysis of interviews with archival research in my discussion, offering a thematic analytical narrative to convey the complex shifts and challenges to the emergence, development, and institutionalization of public relations in Australia. The narrative I construct incorporates secondary sources and research into PRIA state and national archives to validate emergent findings and cross-checks information obtained through interviews with secondary sources and other archives, such as PRIA national and state newsletters, board minutes, and annual reports, as well as contemporaneous newspaper articles. I provide an account of the development of public relations in Australia but avoid reducing the findings to a linear, evolutionary, or progressive narrative. Rather than treating history and historical evidence as a window to the past, a critical history reveals alternative perspectives and underlying ideologies, including those of the historian

(Pearson, 2009). Critical histories interrogate taken-for-granted accounts and official histories (Dean, 1994; L'Etang, 1995). This approach is relevant for this study because I am trying to understand the historical factors that shaped contemporary public relations in Australia.

NOTES

1. Both Macnamara and Crawford (2014) and PRIA (see www.pria.com.au) state PRIA was formed in 1949.

2. Turnbull (2010) cites the increase in Melbourne public relations agencies from 59 in 1976 to 270 ten years later, but offers no source. In contrast, Turner, Bonner, and Marshall (2000) cite 58 (not 59) agencies in 1976 and 270 in 1986, and state they are Australia-wide, not specifically Melbourne agencies. Their source is the annual listing of agencies and consultancies in *B&T* magazine.

3. For further evidence of the unpopularity of the written examination in Western Australia, see Professional Challenge, (1989), where it is noted the take-up was low, and Horne, (1989) in the state council-produced newsletter.

4. PRIA established the College of Fellows on October 1, 1987 (PRIA National Convention, 1990). State institutes had previously used "Fellow" to describe a senior membership category with variable criteria. For example, in the negotiation between AIPR and PRIA (Vic), only one Fellow, a member who "in the opinion of the Council achieved eminence in the profession of Public Relations," could be elected each year (National P.R. Institute, 1956).

5. There is, for instance, evidence of concern over perceived attacks on public relations by the editor of the *West Australian* newspaper and *Scoop*, the AJA's magazine, in the PRIA (WA) newsletter (Allert, 1990).

6. PRIA Board. (1994, November 16). "11. (ii) CAMSA. Other Business," *Minutes of the meeting of the PRIA Board*, p. 6. PRIA (National) archives (ML72/2144, Box 29, Board 93, 94, 95, 97), Mitchell Library, Sydney, Australia.

7. These archives are two files relating to PRIA accreditation rounds (1992–1996 [File 1] and 1997–2001 [File 2]). They belong to Marjorie Anderson, NEC Chair throughout the 1990s, and are on loan to the author. Permission to use the archives was granted on the basis that academics and institutions are not identified.

8. Some participants sought to have their achievements in developing Australian public relations recognized through this research while other participants chose anonymity. My university granted ethics approval on the basis participants could choose whether to be identified.

REFERENCES

Abbott, A. (1988). *The system of professions*. Chicago, IL: University of Chicago Press.

AJA interference threatens PR. (1993, June). *Public Relations: Official Journal of the Public Relations Institute of Australia (NSW)*, pp. 1–2.

AJA log of claims. (1992, May). *Public Relations: Official Journal of the Public Relations Institute of Australia (NSW)*, p. 1.

Allert, J. (1990, April). A critical issue. *Profile: The Newsletter of the Public Relations Institute of Australia (WA)*, p. 3.

Anderson, M. (1990, September). A bigger, brighter, more informative newsletter: Welcome to our inaugural first issue. *Public Relations: Official Journal of the New South Wales and Victorian Branches of the Public Relations Institute of Australia*, p. 1.

Australia's first PR knight. (1971, January/February). *Public Relations Australia*, pp. 8–9.

Breit, R., & Demetrious, K. (2010). Professionalisation and public relations: An ethical mismatch. *Ethical Space: The International Journal of Communication Ethics, 7*(4), 20–29.

Butler, B. (1998). Information subsidies, journalism routines and the Australian media: Market liberalization versus marketplace of ideas. *Prometheus: Critical Studies in Innovation, 16*, 27–45. doi:10.1080/08109029808629251.

Byrne, K. (2008). The value of academia: Variance among academic and practitioner perspectives on the role of public relations academics. *Asia Pacific Public Relations Journal, 9*, 17–34.

Candidates sought for first accreditation exam. (1986, February/March). *Profile: The Newsletter of the Public Relations Institute of Australia (WA)*, p. 1.

Christensen, N. (2014, March 20). PR bosses: PR recruitment agencies and poorly trained uni graduates are a problem. *Mumbrella*. Retrieved from http://mumbrella.com.au/pr-bosses-recruitment-poorly-trained-uni-graduates-problem-215083

Corporates on the way up. (1996, November). *Public Relations: The Newsletter of Public Relations Institute of Australia (NSW, VIC, QLD)*, p. 3.

Crawford, R. (2008). *But wait, there's more … A history of Australian advertising, 1900–2000*. Carlton, Australia: Melbourne University Press.

Crawford, R., & Macnamara, J. (2012). An "outside–in" PR history: Identifying the role of PR in history, culture and sociology. *Public Communication Review, 2*(1), 45–59. Retrieved from http://epress.lib.uts.edu.au/journals/index.php/pcr

Crawford, R., & Macnamara, J. (2014). An agent of change: Public relations in early-twentieth century Australia. In B. St John III, M. O. Lamme, & J. L'Etang (Eds.), *Pathways to public relations: Histories of practice and profession* (pp. 273–289). Abingdon, UK: Routledge.

Davies, C. (1996). The sociology of professions and the profession of gender. *Sociology, 30,* 661–678. doi:10.1177/0038038596030004003.

Davis, M. (2005). Profession and professionalism. In C. Mitcham (Ed.), *Encyclopedia of science, technology and ethics* (Vol. 3, pp. 1515–1519). Detroit, MI: Macmillan Reference USA.

De Bussy, N., & Wolf, K. (2009). The state of Australian public relations: Professionalisation and paradox. *Public Relations Review, 35,* 376–381. doi:10.1016/j.pubrev.2009.07.005.

Dean, M. (1994). *Critical and effective histories: Foucault's methods and historical sociology.* Abingdon, UK: Routledge.

Dell'oso, A-M. (1983, April 29). The psyche of selling: Public relations. *Australian Financial Review: Weekend Review,* pp. 29, 32.

Dwyer, T. (Ed.). (1961). *The Australian public relations handbook.* Melbourne, Australia: Ruskin.

Edwards, L. (2014). Discourse, credentialism and occupational closure in the communications industries: The case of public relations in the UK. *European Journal of Communication, 29,* 319–334. doi:10.1177/0267323113519228.

Edwards, L., & Pieczka, M. (2013). Public relations and "its" media: Exploring the role of trade media in the enactment of public relations' professional project. *Public Relations Inquiry, 2*(1), 5–25. doi:10.1177/2046147X12464204.

Faulconbridge, J., & Muzio, D. (2009). Legal education, globalization, and cultures of professional practice. *The Georgetown Journal of Legal Ethics, 22,* 1335–1359.

First PR accreditation exam planned for October. (1986, February/March). *Profile: The Newsletter of the Public Relations Institute of Australia (WA),* p. 1.

Fitch, K. (2013). A disciplinary perspective: The internationalization of Australian public relations education. *Journal of Studies in International Education, 17,* 136–147. doi:10.1177/1028315312474898.

Fitch, K. (2014a). Professionalisation and public relations education: Industry accreditation of Australian university courses in the early 1990s. *Public Relations Review, 40,* 623–631. doi:10.1016/j.pubrev.2014.02.015.

Fitch, K. (2014b). Perceptions of Australian public relations education, 1985–1999. *Public Relations Inquiry, 3,* 271–291. doi:10.1177/2046147X14535398.

Fitch, K. (2015). Making history: Reflections on memory and "elite" interviews in public relations research. *Public Relations Inquiry, 4*(2), 131–144. doi:10.1177/2046147X15580684.

Fitch, K. (2016). Rethinking Australian public relations history in the mid-twentieth century. *Media International Australia, 160.* doi: 10.1177/1329878X16651135

Fitch, K., & Third, A. (2010). Working girls: Revisiting the gendering of public relations. *Prism, 7*(4). Retrieved from http://www.prismjournal.org/fileadmin/Praxis/Files/Gender/Fitch_Third.pdf

Flower, J. M. (2007). The birth and growth of an information agency. *Asia Pacific Public Relations Journal, 8,* 179–186.

Flower, T. (1988, September 13). Selecting the right PR consultant for the job. *Financial Review: AFR Survey (Public Relations)*, p. 64.

Fontana, A., & Frey, J. H. (2000). The interview: From structured questions to negotiated text. In N. K. Denzin & Y. S. Lincoln (Eds.), *Handbook of qualitative research* (2nd ed., pp. 645–672). Thousand Oaks, CA: Sage.

Freidson, E. (1986). *Professional powers: A study of the institutionalization of formal knowledge.* Chicago, IL: University of Chicago Press.

Gleeson, D. J. (2014). Public relations education in Australia, 1950–1975. *Journal of Communication Management, 18,* 193–206. doi:10.1108/JCOM-11-2012-0091.

Griffen-Foley, B. (2002). Political opinion polling and the professionalisation of public relations: Keith Murdoch, Robert Menzies, and the Liberal Party of Australia. *Australian Journalism Review, 24*(1), 41–59.

Griffen-Foley, B. (2003). A "Civilised Amateur": Edgar Holt and his life in letters and politics. *Australian Journal of Politics and History, 49*(1), 31–47.

Harrison, K. (2011). *Strategic public relations: A practical guide to success.* South Yarra, Australia: Palgrave Macmillan.

Hatherell, W., & Bartlett, J. (2006). Positioning public relations as an academic discipline in Australia. *Asia Pacific Public Relations Journal, 6*(2), 1–13.

Holstein, J., & Gubrium, J. (2008). Constructionist impulses in ethnographic fieldwork. In J. Holstein & J. Gubrium (Eds.), *Handbook of constructionist research* (pp. 373–395). New York, NY: Guildford Press.

Horne, L. (1989, July). Annual report 88/89. *Profile: The Newsletter of the Public Relations Institute of Australia (WA),* p. 4.

Hoy, P., Raaz, O., & Wehmeier, S. (2007). From facts to stories or from stories to facts? Analyzing public relations history in public relations textbooks. *Public Relations Review, 33,* 191–200. doi:10.1016/j.pubrev.2006.11.011.

Hutchinson, J. (1970). *Report on public relations activities, October 1970.* Perth, Australia: Public Works Department, Government of Western Australia.

Hydro-electric commission, Tasmania, has a vacancy for a publicity officer. (1968, February/March). [Advertisement]. *Public Relations Australia,* p. 19.

International P.R. association formed. (1955, August). *P.R. News,* p. 3.

Jabara, L. (1986, September 16). Sound research, high standards vital ingredients for promotions. *Australian Financial Review: Public Relations,* p. 52.

Kaldor, A. G. (1967, July/August). The growth and nature of public relations in Australia. *Public Relations Journal,* pp. 1–8.

King, M. T. (2012). Working with/in the archives. In S. Gunn & L. Faire (Eds.), *Research methods for history* (pp. 13–29). Edinburgh, UK: Edinburgh University Press.

Larson, M. S. (1977). *The rise of professionalism: A sociological analysis.* Berkeley, CA: University of California Press.

L'Etang, J. (1995, July). *Clio among the patriarchs? Historical and social scientific approaches to public relations: A methodological critique.* Paper presented at the meeting of the International Public Relations Symposium, Lake Bled, Slovenia.

L'Etang, J. (1999). Public relations education in Britain: An historical review in the context of professionalisation. *Public Relations Review, 25*(3), 261–289. doi:10.1016/S0363-8111(99)00019-3.

L'Etang, J. (2004). *Public relations in Britain: A history of professional practice in the 20th century.* Mahwah, NJ: Lawrence Erlbaum.

L'Etang, J. (2008a). *Public relations: Concepts, practice and critique.* London, UK: Sage.

L'Etang, J. (2008b). Writing PR history: Issues, methods and politics. *Journal of Communication Management, 12*(4), 319–335. doi:10.1108/13632540810919783.

Macdonald, K. (1995). *The sociology of the professions.* London, UK: Sage.

MacIntosh, I. (1986, September 16). Professionalism heralds new era. *Australian Financial Review: Public Relations,* p. 45.

Mackey, B. (1989, December). Looking back on a dramatic decade. *Profile: The Newsletter of the Public Relations Institute of Australia (WA),* p. 3.

Macnamara, J., & Crawford, R. (2010). Reconceptualising public relations in Australia: A historical and social re-analysis. *Asia Pacific Public Relations Journal, 11*(2), 17–33.

Macnamara, J., & Crawford, R. (2014). Public relations. In B. Griffen-Foley (Ed.), *A companion to the Australian media* (pp. 374–377). North Melbourne, Australia: Australian Scholarly Publishing.

Major plans to strengthen the institute. (1984, September). *Profile: The Newsletter of the Public Relations Institute of Australia (WA),* p. 3.

McKie, D., & Hunt, M. (1999). Staking claims: Marketing, public relations and territories. *Asia Pacific Public Relations Journal, 1*(2), 43–58.

Meet the members. (1956, July/August). *P.R. News, 2*(5), pp. 5–6.

Morath, K. (2008). *Pride and prejudice: Conversations with Australia's public relations legends.* Elanora, Australia: Nuhouse Press.

Muzio, D., & Kirkpatrick, I. (2011). Introduction: Professions and organizations—A conceptual framework. *Current Sociology, 59,* 389–405. doi:10.1177/0011392111402584.

National journal, 1990 report of the PRIA. (1990, November). *Public Relations: Official Journal of the New South Wales and Victorian Branches of the Public Relations Institute of Australia,* p. 4.

National P.R. institute. (1956, September/October). *P.R. News,* p. 8.

New W.A. chapter. (1971, January/February). *Public Relations Australia,* p. 3.

Nicholls, F. (2007). John Matthew Flower [Obituary]. *Asia Pacific Public Relations Journal, 8,* 187–188.

Noordegraaf, M. (2011). Remaking professionals? How associations and professional education connect professionalism and organizations. *Current Sociology, 59*, 465–488. doi:10.1177/0011392111402716.

NSW's "Man of Achievement." (1970, November/December). *Public Relations Australia*, p. 5.

Oral examination, 1990 report of the PRIA. (1990, November). *Public Relations: Official Journal of the New South Wales and Victorian Branches of the Public Relations Institute of Australia*, p. 3.

Parliament of NSW. (n. d.). Sir Asher Alexander JOEL, K.B.E (1912–1998). Retrieved from http://www.parliament.nsw.gov.au/prod/PARLMENT/members.nsf/ec78138918334ce3ca256ea200077f5d/7332d0470aac4794ca256e7f001192be!OpenDocument

Pearson, R. (2009). Perspectives on public relations history. In R. Heath, E. L. Toth, & D. Waymer (Eds.), *Rhetorical and critical approaches to public relations II* (pp. 92–109). New York, NY: Routledge.

Pieczka, M. (2000). Objectives and evaluation in public relations work: What do they tell us about expertise and professionalism? *Journal of Public Relations Research, 12*(3), 211–233. doi:10.1207/S1532754XJPRR1203_1.

Pieczka, M. (2002). Public relations expertise deconstructed. *Media Culture Society, 24*(3), 301–323. doi:10.1177/016344370202400302.

Pieczka, M. (2006). Paradigms, systems theory and public relations. In J. L'Etang & M. Pieczka (Eds.), *Public relations: Critical debates and contemporary practice* (pp. 333–357). Mahwah, NJ: Lawrence Erlbaum.

Pieczka, M. (2007). Case studies as narrative accounts of public relations practice. *Journal of Public Relations Research, 19*, 333–356. doi:10.1080/10627260701402432.

Pieczka, M., & L'Etang, J. (2006). Public relations and the question of professionalism. In J. L'Etang & M. Pieczka (Eds.), *Public relations: Critical debates and contemporary practice* (pp. 265–278). Mahwah, NJ: Lawrence Erlbaum.

Potts, J. D. S. (Ed.). (1976). *Public relations practice in Australia*. Sydney, Australia: McGraw Hill.

Potts, J. D. S. (1986, September 16). Courses satisfy demand for broader professional skills. *Australian Financial Review: Public Relations*, p. 50.

Potts, J. D. S. (2008, November). *Evening with a Fellow*. Paper presented at the meeting of Public Relations Institute of Australia, Sydney, Australia. Retrieved from www.pria.com.au/resources//an-evening-with-a-fellow-david-potts-november-2008

PR industry at the crossroads: Results announced for first-ever survey of P.R. industry. (1985, October). *Profile: The Newsletter of the Public Relations Institute of Australia (WA)*, pp. 1–2.

PRIA national convention an outstanding success. (1990, November). *Public Relations: Official Journal of the New South Wales and Victorian Branches of the PRIA*, p. 5.

Profile: Noel Griffiths. (1965, July/August). *Public Relations Journal*, pp. 6–7.

Public Relations Institute of Australia [PRIA]. (2010). Sir Asher Joel. Retrieved from http://www.pria.com.au/aboutus/in-honour/sir-asher-joel

Putnis, P. (1993). National preoccupations and international perspectives in communication studies in Australia. *The Electronic Journal of Communication, 3*(3&4). Retrieved from http://www.cios.org/EJCPUBLIC/003/3/00333.HTML

Quarles, J., & Rowlings, B. (1993). *Practising public relations: A case study approach.* Melbourne, Australia: Longman Cheshire.

Ray, G. (1990, November). A landmark newsletter. *Public Relations: Official Journal of the New South Wales and Victorian Branches of the Public Relations Institute of Australia*, p. 1.

Reed, M. (1996). Expert power and control in late modernity: An empirical review and theoretical synthesis. *Organization Studies, 17,* 573–597. doi:10.1177/017084069601700402.

Sheehan, M. (2007, November). *Australian public relations campaigns: A select historical perspective 1899–1950.* Paper presented at the meeting of Australian media traditions: Distance and diversity: Reaching new audiences. Bathurst, Australia. Retrieved from http://www.csu.edu.au/special/amt/publication/sheehan.pdf

Sheehan, M. (2010). Eric White. Retrieved from Public Relations Institute of Australia [PRIA]. www.pria.com.au/aboutus/in-honour-2/eric-white

Sheehan, M. (2014a). Foundations of public relations in Australia and New Zealand. In J. Johnston & M. Sheehan (Eds.), *Public relations: Theory and practice* (4th ed., pp. 20–47). Crows Nest, Australia: Allen & Unwin.

Sinclair, J. (2014). Advertising agencies. In B. Griffen-Foley (Ed.), *A companion to the Australian media* (pp. 6–7). North Melbourne, Australia: Australian Scholarly Publishing.

Sparrow, M. (1956, January/February). What we're doing and saying. *P.R. News,* pp. 4–6.

Stanger, J. (1966, January/February). People in public relations. *Public Relations Journal*, p. 4.

Starck, N. (1999). *Accredited or discredited? A qualitative study of public relations education at Australian universities.* Unpublished master's thesis, RMIT, Melbourne, Australia.

Steedman, C. (2002). *Dust: The archive and cultural history.* New Brunswick, NJ: Rutgers University Press.

Suddaby, R., & Viale, T. (2011). Professionals and field-level change: Institutional work and the professional project. *Current Sociology, 59,* 423–442. doi:10.1177/0011392111402586.

Tansey, O. (2007). Process tracing and elite interviewing: A case for non-probability sampling. *PS: Political Science and Politics, 40,* 765–772. doi:10.1017/S1049096507071211.

Tasmania at last. (1967, March/April). *Public Relations Journal*, p. 3.

The professional challenge. (1989, October). *Profile: The Newsletter of the Public Relations Institute of Australia (WA)*, p. 3.

The speakers. (1966, March). Public relations in a shrinking world: March 10–13. *Public Relations Journal*, pp. 11–17.

Thomson, A. (2012). Life stories and historical analysis. In S. Gunn & L. Faire (Eds.), *Research methods for history* (pp. 101–117). Edinburgh, UK: Edinburgh University Press.

Thomson, I. (1956, May/June). Meet the members: No. 2—Asher Alexander Joel OBE. *P.R. News*, pp. 3–6.

To the editor. (1966, July). *Public Relations Journal*, p. 11.

Turnbull, N. (2010). *How PR works—But often doesn't*. Melbourne, Australia: N. S. & J. S. Turnbull. Retrieved from http://noelturnbull.com/wp-content/uploads/2010/06/How-PR-works-but-often-doesnt.pdf

Turner, G. (2002). Public relations. In S. Cunningham & G. Turner (Eds.), *The media and communications in Australia* (pp. 217–225). Crows Nest, Australia: Allen & Unwin.

Turner, G., Bonner, F., & Marshall, P. D. (2000). *Fame games: The production of celebrity in Australia*. Cambridge, NY: Cambridge University Press.

Tymson, C., Lazar, P., & Lazar, R. (2008). *The new Australian and New Zealand public relations manual* (5th ed.). Manly, Australia: Tymson Communications.

Victory in W.A. (1967, September/October). *Public Relations Journal*, p. 11.

WA state council concerned at national accreditation plans. (1985, February). *Profile: The Newsletter of the Public Relations Institute of Australia (WA)*, p. 2.

Ward, I. (1999). The early use of radio for political communication in Australia and Canada: John Henry Austral, Mr Sage and the Man from Mars. *Australian Journal of Politics & History*, 45, 311–330. doi:10.1111/1467-8497.00067.

Ward, I. (2003). An Australian PR state? *Australian Journal of Communication*, 30(1), 25–42.

Watson, T. (2015). What in the world is public relations? In T. Watson (Ed.), *Perspectives on public relations historiography and historical theorization* (pp. 4–19). Houndmills, England: Palgrave Macmillan.

Watson, T., & Macnamara, J. (2013). The rise and fall of IPRA in Australia: 1959 to 2000. *Asia Pacific Public Relations Journal*. Retrieved from http://eprints.bournemouth.ac.uk/21225/

What we're doing and saying. (1955, November–December). *P.R. News*, p. 20.

Wide scope for public relations. (1951, June 15). *The Advertiser*, p. 13.

Witz, A. (1992). *Professions and patriarchy*. London, UK: Routledge.

Zawawi, C. (2009). A history of public relations in Australia. In J. Johnston & C. Zawawi (Eds.), *Public relations: Theory and practice* (3rd ed., pp. 26–46). Crows Nest, Australia: Allen & Unwin.

CHAPTER 2

Education and the Professional Project

Abstract As early as the 1950s, there were competing understandings of the significance of tertiary education as preparation for public relations careers. As the industry developed, tensions emerged between expertise gained through Australian industry practice and an understanding of abstract knowledge gained through university learning. The regulation of education and training, which focused increasingly on the tertiary sector with the introduction of a national course accreditation programme in 1991, remains an important component in the industry's professional drive. This chapter therefore explores the institutionalization of public relations in the academy and the significance for an industry seeking professional recognition. The findings point to the construction of Australian public relations knowledge and the contests around that knowledge that played out in an expanding higher education sector.

Keywords Australia • Accreditation • Education • History • Professionalization • Public relations

© The Editor(s) (if applicable) and The Author(s) 2016   29
K. Fitch, *Professionalizing Public Relations*,
DOI 10.1057/978-1-137-57309-4_2

INTRODUCTION

This chapter investigates the development of public relations as a course of study in the Australian higher education sector, and focuses on social and political contexts and industry attempts to regulate the education and training of future practitioners in the final decades of the twentieth century. It considers the factors, which influenced public relations education and the constitution of knowledge underpinning the public relations curriculum, and reveals tensions and ambiguities around constructions of public relations knowledge and challenges to public relations in the academy. The development of a public relations curriculum offers important insights into the attempts to establish disciplinary boundaries and academic legitimacy as well as the contested understandings of public relations knowledge and expertise. The industry's renewed professionalization drive in the 1980s meant PRIA sought a stronger role in regulating the transmission of that knowledge. This chapter argues that the emergence of public relations in Australian higher education can only be understood in relation to broader societal changes including the massification and increasing vocationalization of Australian higher education.

PUBLIC RELATIONS EDUCATION IN AUSTRALIA

Imagining the Educated Practitioner

From the establishment of professional institutes in the 1950s, practitioners were interested in education and training, and, in particular, university education. One of the early invited speakers to a PRIA (Vic) event was Sir John Medley, who was vice-chancellor of the University of Melbourne from 1938 until 1951 (Serle, 2000). Medley was a highly regarded advocate of education and of post-war reconstruction. Medley reportedly stated "he didn't believe our Universities should establish Chairs in Public Relations as have been done in the U.S. because he said that a thorough education along general lines should fit a man for our profession" (Patterson, 1952). However, not everyone agreed. H.E. Patterson, public relations manager at Claude Mooney Advertising, claimed in a letter to the state president "Public Relations is a highly technical profession and requires a thorough technical training" and that the institute should therefore prioritize encouraging universities to establish a public relations chair (1952, p. 5). In contrast, founding committee member, consultant John Handfield, stated "the kindly and sound advice of a man of Sir John Medley's standing" should not be rejected; public relations did not require a university chair to be a profession; and that not only was public relations not "a highly technical profession" but that it lacked "the theoretical basis of such callings as Medicine, Dentistry or even Law" (1952, pp. 5–6). These contrasting perspectives, reported in only the second PRIA (Vic) newsletter, reveal an early yet persistent theme in relation to public relations education: whether the industry required a generalist education versus technical training for the job.

John Handfield, then owner of Metro Publicity Services and coincidentally joint newsletter editor, embraced the first perspective. In the institute-sponsored *The Australian Public Relations Handbook* (Dwyer, 1961), Handfield argued university education was necessary for future practitioners to gain "breadth of knowledge" rather than vocational training and recommended courses in: "English, political science, history (including Asian history), psychology, economics, economic geography, sciences outside psychology, [and] an introduction to scientific method" along with learning a foreign language, preferably an Asian one (1961, p. 216). Handfield arguably points to a particular kind of Australian cultural capital, as necessary for public relations practice, noting:

A good PR man should have a good background in Australian literature— poetry, art, politics, and particularly Australia's relationship with other countries. Novels as well as books of information should be on the reading list—including novels by Asian authors. (1961, p. 218)

University education was significant not so much in developing a body of knowledge as much as in terms of developing a particular kind of social and cultural capital for industry practitioners. Indeed, in the inaugural PRIA (Vic) newsletter, one definition of public relations was "Good manners to win friends," pointing directly to understandings of class and "gentlemanly" behaviour (Odd Thoughts on PR, 1952). Entry into public relations is often determined by nebulous personal qualities, which L'Etang defined in relation to expertise required to work in the British industry as including "common sense, good manners and 'clubbability,'" contingent on old-boy networks (2004, p. 218). Similarly, Edwards (2014) points to the significance of class and elite networks in largely white, professional groups.

An interest in university-level public relations education was also expressed by members of the Sydney-based AIPR in the early years.

Professor J.F. Clark, a professor of applied psychology, identified the need for specialized training for future executives and argued that "the qualities of character and experience required to pioneer an effort such as the creation of a new profession of Public Relations are quite different from those required to carry it on" (Academic Qualification, 1955, p. 1). In 1955, the AIPR state council identified only one suitable course: the BSc in Applied Psychology at the University of Technology. That course included subjects in Human Relations, Industrial Psychology, and Counselling and could potentially incorporate more content on public relations (Academic Qualification, 1955, p. 2). The same newsletter included a PRSA list of education institutions in the USA that offered public relations degrees.

Two decades later, in a PRIA-supported and -endorsed textbook developed primarily for the growing number of public relations courses at colleges of advanced education and institutes of technology, the PRIA (NSW) state president imagines the future and suggests in 1992 tertiary qualifications will be standard (Myers, 1976). However, he expressed concern about an "overacademic approach," imagining that "economic, psychological jargon and so on [would get] in the way of effective communication" (Myers, p. 329). In the second chapter, "The skills and training of a public relations practitioner," book editor David Potts, who established a diploma in public relations at Mitchell College in 1971, identifies the need for future practitioners to "come from tertiary education courses in public relations in which a broadly-based education is offered in addition to training in communication skills" as "since public relations practitioners are no longer simply publicists, the industry is relying less on journalists for recruits" (1976, p. 17). Potts, who was awarded a Medal of the Order of Australia in 2012 for his service to the public relations profession, most notably to public relations education (PRIA, 2012), remains alert, decades later, to the "real danger, therefore, of having PR taught by academic staff who have little or no real workplace public relations experience," and questions whether the public relations discipline needs fulltime academics (2008, p. 7). Not only is industry practice considered the dominant referent for the public relations body of knowledge to be transmitted in the university sector (Hatherell & Bartlett, 2006), but industry practice is constructed as continuously improving and the site of innovation and knowledge development, whereas academic public relations is constructed as static, and in real danger of becoming "out of touch." This perspective continues to inform contemporary discussions of public relations education.

The Growth in Public Relations Education

Although the Mitchell College course, introduced by David Potts in 1971, is widely identified as the "first" public relations degree course, there is evidence of non-degree public relations short courses, certificate courses, and associate diplomas available through commercial enterprises, private colleges, universities, and other higher education providers prior to the Mitchell College course (Fitch, 2013). For example, the American organization, International Correspondence School, offered courses in advertising, marketing, media selection, and campaign management in many countries, including Australia, as early as 1910 (Ellis & Waller, 2011). From the early post-war years of professional institutes in NSW and Victoria, occasional lectures and short courses were offered by the Australian Institute of Management using senior public relations institute members as lecturers (Dwyer, 1961). The institutes managed their own professional development and training programmes and even created a "student" membership category in the first half of the 1950s, despite the lack of available courses.

Courses in public relations were run by the professional institutes in conjunction with education institutions in the mid-1960s, with the NSW Institute of Technology offering a part-time evening course on public relations over a five-week period in 1965 (Gleeson, 2012, 2014) and the University of New South Wales running a course of ten evening lectures in conjunction with the public relations institute in November and December 1965 and again in February and March 1966 (J. Nolan, personal communication, September 17, 2012; NSW Course, 1965). From the late 1960s, diploma and certificate courses were available at institutes of technology in Victoria, South Australia, and NSW (Public Relations Education, 1966; Gleeson, 2014) and later in Queensland. These courses include a three-year, part-time certificate course at RMIT's School of Management, introduced in 1964, and a three-year diploma course at the South Australian Institute of Technology, introduced in 1967 (Gleeson, 2014; S.A. Course, 1965). These courses were mostly taught by senior practitioners, including senior PRIA members. For example, Eric White Associates (EWA) provided both 32 lectures on public relations techniques and a lecturer to the South Australian Institute of Technology; RMIT courses were taught "under the leadership of various members of the Melbourne Office of Eric White Associates" and the PRIA (Vic) vice president; and the national president and NSW council taught on an extension course offered by the University of New South Wales (Public Relations Education, 1966; Training in S.A., 1967).

PRIA sought significant involvement in the development and regulation of public relations training in part to maintain a jurisdiction over public relations activity. Anderson, the PRIA (NSW) state president in 1990, and NEC chair throughout the 1990s, wrote PRIA "must be in the market because of the shysters that 'float' through with their one day PR certificates!"[1] PRIA's involvement in public relations education was a profitable activity for the PRIA (NSW) state council in the early 1990s, as the council generated revenue through professional development courses (APBC Offers First, 1990; Ray, 1991). The PRIA (NSW) state council collaborated with the Australian Progressive Business College (APBC) in the late 1980s in Sydney to develop a part-time, year-long evening course, and by 1991 the course was full (PRIA [NSW] To Run PR courses, 1990). PRIA members David Potts and John Bulbeck, both former lecturers, ran various courses, including an eight-week introductory course and a 12-month programme; Marjorie Anderson (PRIA state president), David Potts, and Lyn MacIver (a University of Technology Sydney [UTS] lecturer) were on the management committee (APBC Offers First, 1990; Report on Education, 1990).[2] The PRIA (NSW) earned A\$4165 from the arrangement with APBC in 1991 and anticipated earning significantly more the following year (Education Venture's First, 1992).

In addition to Mitchell College, other institutions began to introduce public relations subjects and courses throughout the 1970s and 1980s, partly in response to the sweeping reforms that led to the massification of higher education in Australia. In 1974, RMIT introduced a part-time Certificate in Business Studies (Public Relations) and QIT (now QUT) introduced a three-year Bachelor of Business (Communication). The Western Australian Institute of Technology (WAIT)'s English Department included a single public relations subject in its writing course in 1976 (Potts, 1976). WAIT—later Curtin University—introduced a Bachelor of Business (Public Relations) in their School of Management in 1986, although their School of Social Sciences had introduced a public relations major a few years prior, and Ku-ring-gai College of Advanced Education taught the first graduate course, a graduate diploma in communication management, in 1983 (Quarles & Rowlings, 1993). QIT offered a Master's degree in mass communication, which allowed students to focus on either advertising, electronic and print journalism, or public relations, in 1985 (PR Masters Degree, 1985).

Public relations courses grew increasingly popular with students from the mid- to late 1980s, with reports of significant growth in student numbers. Deakin University doubled enrolment in its Management Communication course, identifying a significant increase from 1987 (Quarles & Potts, 1990). Similar trends were noted at University College of Central Queensland and Charles Sturt University, while UTS received 2000 applications for the 160 places in its communication degree in 1989 (Quarles & Potts, 1990). Other universities reported steady increases in the late 1980s and early 1990s, with one university confirming its student numbers grew from an initial intake of 52 in 1987 to a 1993 intake of 103.[3] Quarles and Rowlings (1993) note the substantial development of tertiary programmes in public relations in the previous decade, particularly in the five years prior to 1992. In the 1990s, along with significant growth in the number of undergraduate courses, the number of postgraduate courses more than doubled. The number of accredited undergraduate and postgraduate public relations courses in Australia doubled in the 1990s, with increasingly specialized courses, in the form of named degrees, on offer.

The Marketization of Higher Education

It was not until the second half of the 1980s that public relations developed significantly as a course of study. The number of tertiary institutions offering public relations increased from 3 to 14 over the decade (Quarles & Potts, 1990). But the establishment of public relations courses needs to be understood in the context of a changing higher education sector, which allowed the development of new fields such as communication studies. Changes in government education policy led to the massification and marketization of higher education. In the 1970s, and in contrast to the more established universities, colleges of advanced education adopted a more utilitarian and vocational focus and introduced more diverse and specialized courses (Fitch, 2013; Maras, 2004; Putnis, 1986; Raciti, 2010). Significantly, public relations became established in the lower status institutes of technology and colleges of advanced education, which became universities with the introduction of the Unified National System in 1987. The introduction of fee-paying international undergraduate students in the same year meant vocationally oriented courses such as public relations became important revenue raisers, and this trend continued into the 1990s as Australian universities became increasingly reliant on income generated by overseas students, with growing demand for social science and business courses from students in Asia (Fitch, 2013; Gallagher, 2011; Raciti, 2010). In response to further government reforms, mergers of existing colleges and institutes in 1996 led to 36 "new" universities that focused primarily on education rather than research (Marginson & Considine, 2000; Raciti, 2010).

The introduction of public relations as a course of study to institutes of technologies and colleges of advanced education in the 1970s, and fuelled in the 1980s by the expansion of both the industry and the higher education sector, follows a similar trajectory to journalism, advertising, and, to a lesser extent, marketing courses (Burns, 2003; Ellis & Waller, 2011; Kerr, Waller, & Patti, 2009). Advertising, for example, was part of the curriculum expansion of new universities, and its growth in universities can be linked to market demand and the rapid growth of the advertising industry in the 1980s (Kerr, Walller, & Patti, 2009). The early development of professional communication courses was strongly influenced by US schools, offering a practical focus on mass communication, an emphasis on empirical research rather than cultural analysis, the unproblematic transmission of messages, and strong links with business education (Lewis, 1982; Putnis, 1986). However, the link between the development of public relations and communication studies in the context of significant changes in the higher education sector in Australia, as well as the growth in communication professions, is under-researched. The majority of public relations programmes in Australia are traditionally taught within communication or arts faculties. For example, in 1990, 12 of the 14 courses with a public relations component in Australia were taught in humanities, social science, or communication schools, and only two courses were offered in business schools (Quarles & Potts, 1990). In contrast, Weaver (2016) notes it is relatively unusual for public relations to be located in media schools in the UK, and public relations was frequently excluded from the evolution of media studies. In North America, public relations tended to be located in journalism schools (Wright, 2011), but its disciplinary alignment was on occasion contested. As chair of the Commission for Public Relations Education, Kruckeberg (1998) argued that as a professional occupation, public relations was not a sub-set of other disciplines such as journalism or mass communication.

By the late 1990s, communication studies was the largest field of study in the humanities in Australia (Putnis & Axford, 2002). Its success is attributed to the need for lower status institutions to expand their offerings through the introduction of new courses and double and postgraduate degrees, following the 1987 Dawkins and 1996 Vanstone reforms to the higher education sector (Borland, 1995; Maras, 2006). In a survey of communication studies courses at 33 tertiary institutions in Australia, Molloy and Lennie (1990) found communication studies was a broad field made up of almost 50 subjects. Many programmes offered pathways to communication professions. The most common professional training in communication studies was journalism, which was offered at 64% of Australian tertiary institutions teaching communication studies, followed by television production (offered at 58% of institutions) and then public relations (offered at 48%, or 16 of the 33 institutions surveyed). According to the report, *Communication Studies in Australia*, approximately 1870 students were studying public relations at undergraduate level in 1990, although these figures were self-reported by the universities (Molloy & Lennie, 1990).

DEFINING AND REGULATING "KNOWLEDGE"

The Early Australian Public Relations Curriculum

Professional institutes expressed persistent concerns about university education, although the nature of concerns shifted as public relations became established as a course of study in the university sector. Originally, the state institutes sought the credibility associated with university learning but associated it either with generalized knowledge and the development of a specific cultural capital or else perceived that universities could offer the specialized training for future practitioners as well as confirm the "scientific" knowledge that underpinned public relations expertise. The professional association's interest in university education is evident in the inclusion of detailed course outlines in newsletters (see S.A. Course, 1965; New Breed of P.R. Man, 1967; Outline of the Mitchell College, 1971). Analysis of these curricula highlights the construction of public relations knowledge, and its transmission through education and training.

The South Australian Institute of Technology planned a three-year, part-time course in public relations following discussions with the state institute (S.A. Course, 1965). The proposed topics included press relations (including press releases, newspaper production, trade journals, and provincial and suburban newspapers), advertising, radio and television, sectorial considerations (i.e., public relations in manufacturing, churches, retail, government, finance, military, fashion, hospitals, and charities), and films, brochures, publications as well as ethics and legal issues. The very first topic listed is "Public Relations is a Top Management Function" (S.A. Course, 1965, p. 3). In addition, students were taught about principles of management, business communication, statistics and economics, and psychology.

The Diploma of Arts (Public Relations) offered at Mitchell College in 1971 shared a common first year with the three-year diploma course in journalism; however, public relations students enrolled in an organization theory subject in lieu of an optional elective. The course can best be described as multidisciplinary in that in first year, students completed individual subjects in English, writing, linguistics, organization theory, and psychology; in second year, students enrolled in English, psychology, political studies, mass communication, and a public relations subject; in their third year, they studied English, public relations, film and video, journalism, and economics. Public relations was therefore only one subject in a very generalist course. In 1974, Mitchell College introduced a Bachelor of Arts through its general studies programme, stating in the handbook the aim is "the provision of courses in applied arts and sciences to prepare students for vocational areas which are relatively new or for which formal training has not been readily available before at tertiary level." Students could choose professional majors in journalism, public relations, or communication. Students enrolled in one communication subject exclusive to their major each semester and were expected to select additional majors from the following disciplines: English, drama, political science, economics, psychology, sociology, history, and geography. In addition, students had to enrol in one sub-major from any of the above, or in legal studies, accountancy, marketing, organizational studies, mathematics, and public administration. Therefore, expectations at Mitchell College for a public relations bachelor course were of a generalist arts education. Students could choose to supplement their studies with more business-oriented units, although this was not compulsory.

In parallel with the significant growth in student numbers, the communications studies curriculum was a topic of major concern for communication studies academics in the mid- to late 1980s. In a discussion paper, Putnis notes that communication studies "provides an organizing focus for input from a number of disciplines usually psychology, sociology, linguistics and cultural studies" (1988, p. 32). Several interview participants acknowledged a fierce resistance by academics in other fields to the introduction of public relations at their institutions, confirming other research into the history of communication studies in Australia (see, for instance, Flew, Sternberg, & Adams, 2007; Maras, 2003). Initially, this resistance was perceived to pit more traditional and scholarly disciplines against "vocational" fields, particularly in the mid-1980s. However, in the 1990s, tensions emerged between co-emergent fields such as journalism and public relations. Most public relations courses were housed within the broad framework of communication studies, alongside co-emergent fields of study, such as journalism, advertising, and media studies, yet public relations met on occasion strong resistance from both more theoretical fields and from emerging fields such as journalism. Participant 4 noted other scholars "hated journalism until public relations came along" but then discussed their experience of opposition from journalism educators: "they had a mission in life to destroy public relations ... they had no respect for public relations." Public relations, at least at Participant 4's university, suffered in terms of its academic legitimacy due to perceptions of its commercial or business orientation. While some participants acknowledged a rivalry with journalism, at many institutions, journalism and public relations courses co-existed within the umbrella discipline of communication studies.

Industry Knowledge and University Education

Some universities—such as Murdoch University in Western Australia—offered a theoretical course focusing on communication studies rather than specific preparation for a career in advertising, public relations, or journalism. Other universities offered students a choice of vocationally oriented subjects as preparation for a professional career in one of these areas, along with a theoretical core of generalist communication units. However, by 1990, several universities were developing public relations units and courses often in conjunction with industry practitioners. In the case of Curtin University, and perhaps to a lesser extent, Western Australian College of Advanced Education (WACAE)/Edith Cowan University (ECU), these units focused on practical skill development to produce job-ready graduates for the industry. With the launch of the Bachelor of Business (Public Relations) at WAIT in 1986, a call was made in the PRIA (WA) newsletter for "experienced practitioners to assist the academic staff with lectures, workshops, seminars and tutorials" (Can You Help, 1986; Public Relations Course, 1986). The article stated that "tertiary qualifications are not necessary" as "the most important attributes ... are experience and skill in one or more aspect of public relations." Another article announces the appointment of "the first full time teacher" for the WAIT course, June Dunstan, whose qualifications included Bachelor of Arts in English with a journalism major and "extensive PR experience" in the not-for-profit and university sectors (June Dunstan Takes, 1986). The PRIA (WA) state council reported that:

> Half of the proposed WAIT course will be devoted to units which are genuine public relations units, including marketing management, consumer behaviour, market research and public relations. The remainder of the course will be split between journalism and management units. (National Council Accredits, 1984)

The business emphasis is not surprising as this particular course was offered in a business school. Nevertheless, in 1984, there appears to be little distinction between public relations and marketing. In 1989, Curtin University recruited an American academic, Dr Gerry Egan, described as "experienced in public relations roles in a variety of organisations," who planned "to structure the Curtin PR course on the basis of practice of skills and involvement with the PR industry," suggesting that industry practice continued to be a significant referent for course design (Curtin Chatter, 1989).

Another Western Australian tertiary institution, WACAE, that later became ECU, developed a humanities course in conjunction with local PRIA members, which included a public relations core of six units in 1990. These units included "a detailed exploration of the theories and models of communication, public relations, management and the psychosocial basis of public relations; the development of practical research, writing, oral presentation, planning and programming skills; the planning and evaluation of public relations applications in a wide variety of contexts; and a case study analysis of public relations in action" (Gae Takes Charge, 1990). In addition, students spent 120 hours in their final semester working in a consultancy or organization as part of a major project. By 1990, some universities were offering more than the broad generalist and interdisciplinary degree as preparation for a communication-related career and attempted to position public relations within communication theory, in contrast to the earlier course developed by WAIT.

There is evidence in PRIA state council archives of significant interaction between universities and their local state councils. For instance, PRIA (WA) newsletters regularly reported on the activities of their state council's tertiary liaison committee, noting in 1990 "how tertiary liaison activities have grown out of all proportion and impose an increasing strain upon the resources of council"; these activities included liaising with course controllers and the student chapters at Curtin University and WACAE; participating in student new member nights; organizing two student days; and hosting Quarles on "her fact-finding visit in relation to the proposed national education policy" (Committee Activities in Brief, 1990). Another article, announcing the appointment of an experienced practitioner to run the public relations course at WACAE, describes course development in conjunction with PRIA through regular meetings of "a PR Advisory Committee comprising both PRIA and WACAE representatives" (Gae Takes Charge, 1990). The PRIA (WA) state council was actively involved in higher education in a number of ways, offering student workshops and paid internships and encouraging students to attend the PRIA state convention (Top Marks, 1989; Top Offers, 1989; Student Workshop Gains, 1989).

Textbooks for Australian Public Relations Education

As discussed in Chapter 1, public relations textbooks, and therefore education, are strongly functionalist and practice-orientated. The Australian textbook market was dominated by US textbooks in the last decades of the twentieth century (Alexander, 2004; Johnston & Macnamara, 2013; Petelin, 2005). According to Quarles and Potts, educators were forced to supplement Tymson and Sherman's (1987) *The Australian Public Relations Manual* "with American texts, which in themselves are not satisfactory because of the dominance of US case examples" due to its lack of theory (1990, p. 27). Quarles and Potts (1990) identified US textbooks commonly used in Australian public relations courses as *Managing Public Relations* (Grunig & Hunt, 1984); *Effective Public Relations* (Cutlip, Center, & Broom, 1985); and *Experts in Action* (Cantor & Burger, 1984). NEC member and university lecturer Gael Walker (1991), as editor of an inaugural newsletter for public relations educators, reported *Public Relations as Communication Management* (Crable & Vibbert, 1986) was "particularly useful," but that it could only be purchased from the USA as there was no Australian distributor. The dearth of Australian resources was considered by educators and practitioners to be problematic.

Other problems, also identified in the previous chapter, include the uncritical reproduction of existing industry accounts and professional narratives, which confirm the field's professional standing and status as a strategic management discipline. It is perhaps not surprising given the majority of Australian public relations textbooks, at least until 2000, were written mostly by practitioners (often senior PRIA members) and endorsed or in some cases even initiated by PRIA (see Dwyer, 1961; Potts, 1976; Tymson & Sherman, 1987). There is no doubt that this strong practitioner focus was perceived as a strength by many in the industry. Potts later said of his edited book, *Public Relations Practice in Australia*, "unlike many American books written by academics, this volume has been written by practising public relations professionals" (2008, p. 5). However, there were a number of early public relations manuals or handbooks, aimed at, and written by, practitioners such as *The Australian Public Relations Handbook* (Dwyer, 1961). Similar books aimed at practitioners were published in later decades (see, e.g., Mathews, 1984; Macnamara, 1984, 1992, 1996, 2000).

PRIA commissioned *Public Relations Practice in Australia* (Potts, 1976) in the mid-1970s to serve as both a textbook and to promote what public relations could offer to senior managers. In the foreword, the PRIA national president notes that in the context of a broader scope for public relations activity and the increasing demand for specialist communicators, "it is ... a logical and proper responsibility of the Public Relations Institute of Australia ... to support the production of a new and up-to-date book"; its aim is not "to produce solely a how-to-do-it book, but rather one that combines practical information with reasoning" and "to promote two-way communication" (Plater, 1976, p. iv). Scholars note the widespread influence of this book in the Australian education sector, and that it drew heavily on US textbooks, in particular Cutlip and Center (1971) (Johnston & Macnamara, 2013). The 31 chapters were written by high-profile practitioners, many of whom were former or serving PRIA councillors, state presidents, or national presidents. The book offers insights into the way the industry constituted public relations knowledge. The 26 chapters cover topics such as public opinion; attitude research; public relations planning and administration; media relations; films; exhibitions and displays; graphics and photography; and public relations in a range of sectors include corporate, financial, staff and employee, political, international, and marketing public relations. The textbook offers a comprehensive insight into the public relations-specific knowledge the industry, through PRIA, considered necessary for future practitioners to gain, alongside, or as part of, a broad-based, general university education. This knowledge is functionalist; for example, the subheadings under "Administration of a PR consultancy" include "check the credit risk," "tally the time," "selling your services," "assessing a fee," "keeping control," and "budgeting" (Sherman & Griffin, 1976, pp. 80–83).

Another Australian textbook was not produced until 1987. It was written by two practitioners and PRIA members, Candy Tymson and Bill Sherman. Following Sherman's retirement, Tymson produced new editions with high-profile practitioners and father–son team Peter and Richard Lazar (Johnston & Macnamara, 2013). In total, there have been five editions of *The Australian and New Zealand Public Relations Manual*, with the most recent published in 2008. Its focus has remained practical. Quarles and Rowlings's (1993) book, produced in the early 1990s, was unusual in a number of ways. It was co-written by an academic and a senior practitioner, both of whom were active in the PRIA (Vic) state council. Dr Jan Quarles, an American public relations educator, worked in Australia from 1989 to 1994. She was also a member of the NEC in the early 1990s and played a key role in the industry accreditation of university courses. The book foregrounds Australia's relationship with Asia; presumably, it was informed both by Quarles's undergraduate degree in Asian Studies and Australian industry engagement with the Asian region. The second chapter focuses specifically on the need for cultural competence in public relations practitioners, and subsequent chapters include case studies from Australia, Europe, and Asia. The book, written for the Australian market, has a notably global focus. It was not until this century that a more academic textbook was produced. Scholars describe Johnston and Zawawi's (2000) textbook, *Public Relations: Theory and Practice*, as "the first substantial book collection by local writers that was more than a basic manual" (Petelin, 2005, p. 461) and the first textbook to "set a standard in having enough diverse authors and a marketing strategy able to compete with US textbooks in their country of origin" (McKie, 2012, p. 110).

The State of Public Relations Education

With the expansion of the Australian higher education sector, the relationship between industry and the academy changed, and industry bodies in a number of fields sought a significant role in defining university curricula through accreditation processes (Walkington & Vanderheide, 2008). The regulation of public relations education was an important component of PRIA's professional drive. In 1989, the PRIA national board funded a benchmark study into the state of public relations education in Australia and commissioned as authors US academic Quarles, who was teaching at RMIT, and Potts, a senior practitioner and educator who developed the Mitchell College diploma course, taught public relations at both Ku-ring-gai College of Advanced Education and Mitchell College, and had spent sabbaticals at universities in the USA. At the time of writing the report, Potts had returned to industry and was working as a consultant. The report aimed "to provide a base of information for educational institutions" and focused on "the collation of information and research surrounding public relations education, its history, current trends and also the availability and types of resources" (Greenmount, 1990).

The 1990 report, *Public Relations Education in Australia*, drew on in-depth interviews with public relations educators, questionnaires, and supporting materials and found 14 higher education courses where public relations was taught as a major, minor, or subject option. Ten courses were accredited; there is little information available as to what this accreditation involved, but state-based PRIA councils, and subsequently the PRIA national board, endorsed public relations courses. Nineteen educators were employed on a fulltime basis, "with the most common profile being experience as a practitioner and a B.A. in communications or a related discipline" (Quarles & Potts, 1990, p. 32). Significantly, the report acknowledged the influence of US public relations education and scholarship and the widespread use of US textbooks, but recognized limitations with American approaches in the Australian context. In the same year, IPRA produced a report investigating global standards for public relations education that expressed "alarm [at] the proliferation of universities proclaiming their competence in public relations teaching and research without adequate resources" (1990, p. 5). IPRA recognized the challenge in developing accreditation criteria for public relations courses was "defining the body of knowledge upon which the criteria should be based," given the lack of "all-embracing theory" and "conceptual framework" (IPRA, 1990, p. 25). The Quarles and Potts (1990) report makes specific recommendations for university courses, with the inclusion of an appendix, "Guidelines for the accreditation of courses in public relations at Australian tertiary institutions." The authors point to the lack of Australian research into public relations education and training, and acknowledge that these guidelines are "an adaptation to Australian conditions of research done in recent years by the Public Relations Society of America (PRSA) and educators to determine the content of PR sequences at American colleges and universities" (Quarles & Potts 1990, p. 47). The guidelines identify the need for public relations courses to cover writing, research, and evaluation, strategic planning and management skills, internships, industry advisory committees, and business subjects (Quarles & Potts, 1990). These recommendations became the basis of the formal accreditation criteria for PRIA, following the establishment of the NEC in 1990. Despite several revisions to accreditation criteria in the intervening period, these recommendations continue to inform PRIA accreditation guidelines and the design of university courses seeking industry accreditation.

At various points in the 1980s and 1990s, a number of professional associations expressed an interest in accrediting public relations courses. In addition to efforts to represent public relations practitioners, as well as journalists, as discussed in Chapter 1, the AJA also sought to accredit university public relations courses (AJA Interference, 1993; AJA Log of Claims, 1992). Another organization, the Australian Institute of Professional Communicators, also planned to accredit courses and award scholarships (Starck, 1999, p. 156). However, PRIA resisted and indeed contested attempts by other associations to accredit public relations courses and sought to maintain its jurisdiction over the industry accreditation of university courses.

Industry Accreditation of University Courses

The PRIA National Board established the NEC in 1990 and introduced a formal system of industry accreditation in 1991 partly in response to concerns about the low professional status of the public relations industry, inconsistency in state decision-making in relation to course accreditation, and the significant growth in both the number of courses and students (Fitch, 2014). Until then, individual states accredited courses, but the process was often haphazard. For example, in one state, the state council and the national council only became aware they have previously accredited a course at a competing school at the same university several years prior to the introduction of a national accreditation programme when they accredited a course in the business school.[4] The NEC introduced standardized criteria, "Guidelines for the accreditation of courses in public relations at Australian tertiary institutions" (PRIA, 1991), based on recommendations in the PRIA-commissioned report into Australian public relations education (Quarles & Potts, 1990). These criteria acknowledged the previously inconsistent accreditation of public relations courses and were explicit about the role of education as "the means to pass [the public relations body of knowledge] on to future generations of practitioners" (Quarles & Potts, 1990, p. 46; PRIA, 1991, p. 2). Accreditation was designed for university courses that offered a major in either public relations or organizational communication and the guidelines mandated "no more than 25 per cent of a total course at undergraduate level should be in professional communication/public relations subjects," with the remainder of the course made up of "areas which support the professional core" (Quarles & Potts, 1990, p. 48; PRIA, 1991, p. 4). These supporting areas could include a range of established disciplines, in order to provide a broad education: "aimed at developing the intellectual and problem-solving capacities of students as well as giving a sound understanding of the theory and practice of communication and public relations" (PRIA, 1991, p. 3). The original criteria acknowledged that "arts and sciences remain a strong basis for helping practitioners to understand an increasingly complex world and their role as communicators, and for developing critical faculties" (Quarles & Potts, 1990, p. 3).

The shift to a single NEC led to tensions within PRIA. Contested understandings of the role of education, as either suitable training to meet industry requirements or as an academic discipline offering a broad generalist education, emerged (Fitch, 2014). PRIA National Board reports and minutes record senior practitioner concerns that university courses failed to meet industry needs. The College of Fellows wanted their expertise as senior practitioners with a unique understanding of the Australian context, in contrast to American academics, to be better recognized and sought a greater role in university education (Fitch, 2014). Practitioners preferred business subjects to other disciplines (PRIA, 1991; Quarles & Potts, 1990), despite the location of most Australian courses in humanities or communication rather than business schools, and wanted less emphasis on communication and public relations theory.

The accreditation criteria for the second five-year round, which covered 1997–2001, were revised and included a new section on "minimum standards" and a "guiding philosophy" (PRIA, 1996). Firstly, university education should develop in students a capacity for critical thinking and problem-solving skills to assist with students' future career development. Second, technical—rather than strategic—skills should be taught to assist graduates in their first jobs. Responsibility for the initial review and assessment of university submissions rested with state-based education committees rather than the NEC. It is not clear if the devolution to state-based practitioner committees was in response to concerns expressed at national board meetings around the suitability of graduates of accredited courses. State panels, established specifically to review university submissions for accreditation, were drawn from state education committees, if they existed, or PRIA state councils and members. These committees reviewed university submissions, before reporting their recommendations to the NEC. Universities and their industry advisory committees had the opportunity to comment on the state review panels' recommendations prior to the NEC making a final decision about accreditation.

PROFESSIONALIZATION AND INSTITUTIONALIZATION

Valuing Professional Knowledge

The expectation that university courses should address industry needs resulted in practitioners on PRIA state panels demanding students develop the knowledge they perceived necessary in job-ready graduates. As such, practitioner understandings of education drew on their expectations of employees, effectively defining their understanding of public relations knowledge. Practitioners value years of industry experience, rather than university education (van Ruler, 2005) and perceive that experience as constituting expert knowledge (Pieczka, 2002). One panel stated a university's promoted course outcome—that graduates would have "enough expertise in public relations decision-making to be able to move into consulting work or public relations management"—was too ambitious and noted graduates require a lot of "hand-holding before they are able to claim expertise in public relations decision-making."[5] From the practitioner perspective, then, this expertise, constituted in industry practice, should significantly inform the public relations curriculum; at the same time, precisely because such knowledge was understood to be constituted in practice, universities were unable to effectively develop this expertise in the academic environment.

The incorporation of practitioner perspectives into the public relations curriculum and the recognition of senior PRIA members as experts were critical to PRIA's assessment of university accreditation submissions. One panel identified the lack of academic "staff with industry experience" as a problem and suggested the NEC explain to the university "how other universities run visiting speaker programs … or [have] in residence a local practitioner."[6] Many practitioners on state panels sought greater involvement with their local universities. For example, one chair wrote to the NEC: "the committee has asked me to discuss the accreditation guidelines—the group has some ideas for development e.g. face to face reviews and meeting with students."[7] If university submissions were unsuccessful, most state committees, as well as the NEC, offered to work with the university to redevelop the public relations course.

An example of how industry expectations influenced panels' views of education was the issue of work experience. Although "a practicum/internships/work experience component should be mandatory" and was considered in the written guidelines "to be most beneficial … late in the course" (PRIA, 1991, p. 4; PRIA 1996, p. 3), one panel demanded a university introduce "the additional component of a two-week work experience placement in a public relations environment during the first year of the course."[8] The state education committee "plann[ed] a promotion of the Internship and Work experience programs" and was confident the industry could accommodate additional placements. Although the university's advisory committee chair questioned the wisdom of mandatory placements for first year students, the state education committee was adamant accreditation would be withheld unless the university agreed.[9] Given this demand was not made of universities in other states, considerable leeway was given to state panels in the late 1990s to develop their own processes around industry accreditation, even if their expectations were not strictly in line with the written accreditation criteria.

The 1996 accreditation guidelines are more specific than the 1991 guidelines regarding the qualifications and experience of public relations educators. As in the first national accreditation round, educators were expected to hold a bachelor-level degree, have significant professional experience, and continue their professional development "by work in practice, by consulting, by research and by participation in professional organisations" (PRIA, 1991, p. 6; PRIA, 1996, p. 5). However, in the updated criteria, the course coordinator was also expected to be "a full-time, senior academic … with an undergraduate degree with a major in public relations … have a higher degree, or be working towards a higher degree, in the communications field … and extensive practical experience in public relations practice" (PRIA, p. 5). In practice, this expectation did exist in relation to the first round, but was not explicit in the 1991 criteria (Fitch, 2014a). Anderson supported at least two university lecturers' applications for promotion to professorial positions without a PhD, writing to universities: "that an appropriate Masters degree is a sufficient qualification for an appointment at the Associate Professor level."[10] From the industry perspective, senior appointments in the academy, based on professional experience in industry rather than on traditional academic expectations around scholarly research, would assist in improving the professional standing of public relations.

Defining the Curriculum

Analysis of state panels' reports to the NEC offers insights into panel members' concerns that universities should address industry expectations and needs. These expectations did not necessarily align with PRIA accreditation guidelines, but there is little evidence of the NEC not supporting state panel recommendations. Panels drew on their professional experiences to provide explicit feedback regarding the suitability of courses such as recommending the development of new units on: "government relations and organisation structures"[11] and that one unit be rewritten to so that "students learn ... the role of the media as gatekeepers."[12]

In contrast to the first accreditation round, expectations of an appropriate curriculum were more functionalist. Concern about the development of writing skills, for example, was common feedback to universities, and courses were not accredited until universities agreed to include units on public relations writing.[13] State panels maintained "universities have a responsibility to meet industry requirements in this area."[14] One university, whose accreditation submission was successful, was nevertheless directed to address the lack of "adequate business focus as it is essential that graduates are able to write business letters, proposals, reports and submissions."[15]

Panels recommended textbooks to universities and often specified US textbooks. For example, one panel recommended "that at least one of the Grunig texts be included as essential reading in the program."[16] Feedback included concerns about "the small number of texts (published after 1990) on the reading list"[17] and directions for the university library to "significantly increase—possibly to triple—over the next three years its reference resources with contemporary publications relevant to the Australian business environment."[18] A recurrent theme was the need for more Australian case studies. Feedback regarding international public relations was not consistent. One university was informed a more global, rather than an Asian, focus was required,[19] while another university was directed to rewrite a media unit to "include Japan (as one of Australia's most significant trading partners)."[20]

Developing Disciplinary Boundaries

The proliferation in courses in the 1990s led to more named degrees, such as bachelor's or master's of Communication, rather than generic arts degree courses, as well as graduate and postgraduate diplomas. Typically, universities submitted multiple courses for consideration for accreditation, with some institutions submitting up to five or six undergraduate and postgraduate courses. One university submitted a Public Affairs course; although the state-based education committee thought a course in public affairs was "a good idea," they did not consider it met PRIA accreditation requirements.[21] Analysing the responses to university submissions offers some insights into the ways PRIA, through its various education committees, defined the emerging disciplinary boundaries for public relations within the academy. Ongoing demarcation disputes and threats of encroachment appeared to influence PRIA committee responses. Correspondence suggests many "newer" fields of study were converging in the mid- to late 1990s in terms of course structure; one university, for example, reported a common first year for advertising, marketing, and public relations students,[22] and universities offered both public relations and journalism within communication studies courses. From the industry perspective, journalism education was not adequate training for future public relations practitioners, in that it "lacked the strategic side of public relations" and "journalism is one-way communication."[23] The emphasis on public relations as a strategic management discipline meant that links with journalism and media relations were minimized. For example, one university's submission for a Bachelor of Arts (Mass Communication) was rejected for being "too media focused," and the state panel chair noted the course was "cobbled together from existing units in marketing, media and mass communication."[24]

Although the majority of Australian universities taught public relations within communication studies, state accreditation panels encouraged a greater focus on marketing and business, considering these disciplines offered a better preparation for careers in public relations than, for example, journalism and media studies. Both the 1991 and the 1996 guidelines state practitioners' preference for business studies as part of the 75% of support studies outside the professional core (PRIA, 1991, p. 3; PRIA, 1996, p. 4), with universities encouraged to enrol students in business units as electives.[25] State panels also requested universities include more management content in the public relations curriculum "such as project management, people management, consultancy management, etc."[26] The accreditation guidelines specifically position public relations as a management activity (PRIA, 1991; PRIA, 1996), confirming the professional standing of public relations was perceived to rely on its recognition as a management discipline.

Panels sought a stronger focus on marketing in public relations courses, despite the potential rivalry between marketing and public relations. One panel withheld reaccreditation of one course until the university addressed "the need for a *stronger marketing perspective*" and "emphasise[d] the role of public relations in the marketing mix." [27] It is worth noting that these concerns regarding a stronger marketing orientation were not consistent across different state panels. The accreditation criteria note that although "students in marketing degree courses often take units in public relations as minor studies," such courses will not be considered for accreditation (PRIA, 1996, p. 1). However, senior PRIA members worked in both marketing and public relations roles; Anderson, for instance was an Associate Fellow of the Australian Marketing Institute and Vice President of CAMSA at the same time she was a member of PRIA National Board, NEC chair, and PRIA's Executive Director.[28] There were mixed understandings by PRIA members regarding public relations and marketing; some accepted that the two fields overlapped or complemented each other in practice, while others maintained public relations and marketing were unique and separate. In 1996, a special issue of PRIA's national journal, *The PRofessional*, was devoted to marketing communication; the editor noted "marketing communication was an integral part of public relations" (Berryman, 1996, p. 4), and various authors attest to the importance of public relations in marketing (Factor, 1996; Williams, 1996).

PRIA PERSPECTIVES ON PUBLIC RELATIONS EDUCATION

In the 1990s, PRIA increasingly emphasized practitioner expertise; more practitioner involvement in university education; and stronger expectations that universities should develop suitable employees for the public relations workforce. This last point is significant in that universities were expected to offer suitable training for future employees. That is, in comparison with the first accreditation round, introduced in 1991, when value was placed on an arts degree or generalist education by the NEC, the various PRIA committees sought a more pragmatic outcome from university public relations education, and appeared less concerned with the need for a general and broad university-level education. Indeed, state panel members preferred a stronger business or management orientation in degree courses despite the location of most Australian public relations courses in communication studies.

With the partial devolution to state-based, practitioner committees, there appears to be greater intervention and direction given to universities. This shift marginalized NEC efforts earlier in the decade to promote scholarly endeavours for public relations, in favour of a greater focus on practitioners' concerns, needs, and expectations of public relations education. Ironically, there was a significant increase in critical public relations scholarship in Australia in the second half of the 1990s, exemplified in the publication of a special issue of the *Australian Journal of Communication* in 1995 (Petelin, 2005; L'Etang, 2009) and the launch of the *Asia Pacific Public Relations Journal* in 1999. However, practitioner concerns meant there was a clear expectation that universities would prepare students for industry practice. In contrast, in the second round, universities were given specific advice regarding curriculum content, over and above PRIA (1996) accreditation guidelines. Often advice regarding curricula was based on practitioner perceptions of industry requirements and expertise; for example, panels identified the need for better writing skills; business and management skills; stronger marketing perspectives; an understanding of the media as "gatekeepers"; or of Japan, as Australia's biggest trading partner.

In the second accreditation round, the NEC endorsed the recommendations of state review panels whose expectations of education emerged from an understanding of public relations expertise drawn primarily from industry practice. The value placed on practical experience is illustrated by the demand of one state panel for compulsory work experience for first year students, despite not being a formal requirement. Another example is expectations around the active involvement of practitioners in public relations education, through course advisory committees, guest lectures, workshops, internship programmes, and even through "practitioner-in-residence" and "visiting eminent practitioner" programmes. Although ongoing industry liaison and the existence of a course advisory committee were features of both accreditation rounds, the expectations around industry engagement are greater in the later round, particularly around work experience and socialization for students into public relations practice.

These findings confirm that for many PRIA members involved in education committees, public relations knowledge was constituted in industry practice rather than in universities, echoing the findings of UK studies (Pieczka, 2002, 2007). Writing on education, US scholar Kruckeberg noted that "public relations as a *professional* occupation is ideological" and that professional perspectives must therefore "take precedence over academic unit perspectives and biases" (1998, p. 245). In seeking to establish public relations as a profession, practitioner-led state panels valued a greater business and marketing focus in public relations courses and sought to minimize links with journalism or media studies. Within the academy, however, the proliferation of communication studies courses at both undergraduate and postgraduate levels meant some degree of convergence with advertising, media studies, and journalism courses. Beyond the Anderson archives, there is evidence of growing dissatisfaction within PRIA in the 1990s of university-level education and its capacity to meet industry expectations.

CONCLUSION

This chapter identifies a schism between practical and theoretical public relations knowledge, resulting in a contest over the constitution of public relations knowledge, which I argue played out over, and continues to resonate in contemporary discussions around, public relations education. However it is important to acknowledge the broader social context in which public relations became established as a course of study in higher education. Widespread changes in the Australian education sector, in response to changes in government policy and funding resulted in the expansion of higher education, and the need for new and less established institutions to find diverse markets, primarily through the introduction of more vocational courses. After 1987, new markets were found in international undergraduate students and through increased offerings in postgraduate courses. This chapter argues communication studies provided a disciplinary home and, to an extent, legitimized public relations in the academy in that it aligned public relations with a number of communication industries, including journalism and advertising, and offered opportunities for the scholarly development of public relations. However, the competitive jostling with other co-emergent fields of study contributed to demarcatory and territory disputes in the academy.

Early Australian public relations courses offered a broad, general education mostly focused on a liberal arts education, and occasionally included more business-oriented subjects. In the 1970s, public relations was often a single unit or subject taught within a broader, interdisciplinary course. The growth in communication studies led to the introduction of media and communication units in public relations curricula in later decades. This chapter offers evidence of PRIA's desire to regulate public relations education and training, and to both define and regulate the transmission of public relations knowledge through the establishment of the NEC and the introduction of a standardized, national accreditation programme for university courses in 1991. This knowledge was not fixed and subject to a number of challenges from within the academy and various committees of the professional association. An important finding in this chapter is that Australian public relations education developed in response to the Australian social and political context, and while the professional association, often drawing on US textbooks and guidelines, sought to play a pivotal role in education, their influence on curricula and pedagogy is uncertain.

NOTES

1. Anderson, M. (1991, June 2). [Letter to Tony Stevenson]. Anderson archives (File 1). Professor Stevenson of the Communication Centre at QUT was commissioned by PRIA around 1990 to investigate the future of public relations; the report was never made publicly available (Gleeson, 2012; Quarles & Rowlings, 1993
2. Potts, Anderson, and MacIver also served on the NEC from 1991.
3. University. (1993, April 26). "Application for chair in public relations" [Letter to UK university, copied to Marjorie Anderson]. Anderson archives (File 1).
4. Anderson, M. (n.d.). [Memorandum to NEC, copied to John Malone and state presidents]; and University. (1992, December 16) [Letter to Marjorie Anderson]. Anderson archives (File 1).
5. University (1999, March 31), "B. Comm PR Accreditation" [Email to PRIA National Secretariat]. Anderson archives (File 2).
6. State accreditation committee. (1998, November 9). "Accreditation of tertiary courses in public relations" [Report to NEC]. Anderson archives (File 2).
7. Chair, state accreditation committee. (1998, April 26). [Email to Marjorie Anderson, no subject]. Anderson archives (File 2).

8. Anderson. M. (1997, March 13). [Letter to university, no subject]. Anderson archives (File 2).
9. Chair, university course advisory committee. (1997, April 19). [Letter to NEC, no subject]. Anderson archives (File 2).
10. Anderson, M. (2001, July 26). "To the promotions committee re [lecturer]" [Facsimile to university]. Anderson archives (File 2).
11. Vice president, state council. (1998, March 30). "PRIA accreditation of tertiary course in public relations" [Facsimile and State Accreditation Panel Report (report dated 23 March 1998)]. Anderson archives (File 2).
12. Anderson, M. (1997, March 13). [Letter to university, no subject]. Anderson archives (File 2).
13. Anderson, M. (1998, May 15). "Accreditation of courses in public relations at Australian tertiary institutions" [Letter to university]. Anderson archives (File 2).
14. Vice president, PRIA state council. (1998, March 30). "Accreditation of tertiary courses in public relations" [Facsimile (cover sheet and accreditation panel report) to M. Anderson]. Anderson archives (File 2).
15. Anderson, M. (1999, April 20). "Accreditation of courses in public relations at Australian tertiary institutions" [Letter to university]. Anderson archives (File 2).
16. Anderson, M. (1999, April 20). "Accreditation of courses in public relations at Australian tertiary institutions" [Letter to university]. Anderson archives (File 2).
17. Anderson, M. (1998, March 13). [Letter to university, no subject]. Anderson archives (File 2).
18. Anderson, M. (1997, July 22). "Accreditation of courses in public relations at Australian tertiary institutions" [Letter to university]. Anderson archives (File 2).
19. Anderson, M. (1999, April 20). "Accreditation of courses in public relations at Australian tertiary institutions" [Letter to university]. Anderson archives (File 2).
20. Anderson, M. (1997, March 13). [Letter to university, no subject]. Anderson archives (File 2).
21. Chair, state accreditation committee (1998, April 26). [Email to M. Anderson, no subject]. Anderson archives (File 2).
22. University. (1996, July 26). [Letter to M. Anderson, no subject]. Anderson archives (File 2).
23. [State] accreditation panel. (1998, November 9). "Accreditation of tertiary courses in public relations" [Report to NEC]. Anderson archives (File 2).
24. National education committee. (1999, April 15). Minutes. National Education Committee Teleconference, Anderson archives (File 2); Chair, state tertiary accreditation committee (1999, April 12). "Email for Marjorie Anderson." Anderson archives (File 2).

25. Executive officer, state PRIA council. (1999, December 2). "Re: [university] accreditation" [Letter to M. Anderson]. Anderson archives (File 2).
26. Anderson, M. (1998, June 9). "Accreditation of courses in public relations at Australian tertiary institutions" [Letter to university]. Anderson archives (File 2).
27. Anderson, M. (1997, June 1). "Accreditation of public relations courses" [Letter to university]. Anderson archives (File 2).
28. Anderson, M. (n.d.), "Marjorie Anderson, M. App. Sc. Comm Mgmt, FPRIA" [One-page biography for Anderson on Anderson-Knight letterhead]. Anderson archives (File 2).

REFERENCES

Academic qualification for public relations. (1955, April). Is it coming? A university professor's view. *P.R. News*, pp. 1–2.

AJA interference threatens PR. (1993, June). *Public Relations: Official Journal of the Public Relations Institute of Australia (NSW)*, pp. 1–2.

AJA log of claims. (1992, May). *Public Relations: Official Journal of the Public Relations Institute of Australia (NSW)*, p. 1.

Alexander, D. (2004). Changing the public relations curriculum: A new challenge for educators. *Prism*, *2*(1). Retrieved from www.prismjournal.org/number_2_1.html

APBC offers first intermediate duration PR course. (1990, November). *Public Relations: Official Journal of the New South Wales and Victorian Branches of the Public Relations Institute of Australia*, p. 15.

Berryman, R. (1996). Editor's note. *The PRofessional: Issues on Communication, Corporate Affairs and Public Relations* [Special Issue: Marketing Communication], *1*(4), 4.

Borland, H. (1995). Contested territories and evolving academic cultures: Whither communication studies? *Australian Journal of Communication, 22*(1), 14–30.

Burns, L. S. (2003). Reflections: Development of Australian journalism education. *Asia Pacific Media Educator, 14*, 57–75. Retrieved from http://ro.uow.edu.au/apme/vol1/iss14/5

Can you help with the course? (1986, January). *Profile: The Newsletter of the Public Relations Institute of Australia (WA)*, p. 2.

Cantor, B., & Burger, C. (Eds.). (1984). *Experts in action: Inside public relations.* New York, NY: Longman.

Committee activities in brief: Tertiary liaison. (1990, July). *Profile: The Newsletter of the Public Relations Institute of Australia (WA)*, p. 3.

Crable, R. E., & Vibbert, S. L. (1986). *Public relations as communication management.* Edina, MN: Bellwether Press.

Curtin chatter. (1989, October). *Profile: The Newsletter of the Public Relations Institute of Australia (WA)*, p. 3.

Cutlip, S., & Center, A. H. (1971). *Effective public relations* (4th ed.). Englewood Cliffs, NJ: Prentice Hall.

Cutlip, S., Center, A. H., & Broom, G. M. (1985). *Effective public relations* (6th ed.). Englewood Cliffs, NJ: Prentice Hall.

Dwyer, T. (Ed.). (1961). *The Australian public relations handbook.* Melbourne, Australia: Ruskin.

Education venture's first financial return. (1992, February). *Public Relations: Official Journal for PRIA (NSW)*, pp. 1, 5.

Edwards, L. (2014). *Power, diversity and public relations.* London, UK: Routledge.

Ellis, R. B., & Waller, D. S. (2011). Marketing education in Australia before 1965. *Australasian Marketing Journal, 19*, 115–121. doi:10.1016/j.ausmj.2011.03.003.

Factor, N. (1996). Adding people related skills to the marketing mix. *The PRofessional: Issues on communication, corporate affairs and public relations* [Special Issue: Marketing Communication], *1*(4), 11–12.

Fitch, K. (2013). A disciplinary perspective: The internationalization of Australian public relations education. *Journal of Studies in International Education, 17*, 136–147. doi:10.1177/1028315312474898.

Fitch, K. (2014). Professionalisation and public relations education: Industry accreditation of Australian university courses in the early 1990s. *Public Relations Review, 40*, 623–631. doi:10.1016/j.pubrev.2014.02.015.

Flew, T., Sternberg, J., & Adams, D. (2007). Revisiting the "media wars" debate. *Australian Journal of Communication, 34*(1), 1–27.

Gae takes charge at WACAE. (1990, March). *Profile: The Newsletter of the Public Relations Institute of Australia (WA)*, p. 3.

Gallagher, M. (2011, April). *Envisioning the future global positioning of Australia in education, training and research.*, Paper presented at the meeting of International Education Research Policy Symposium, Melbourne, Australia. Retrieved from http://www.lhmartininstitute.edu.au/documents/publications/gallagherenvisioningpaper.pdf

Gleeson, D. J. (2012). *Revisiting the foundations of public relations education in Australia.* Retrieved from Public Relations Institute of Australia [PRIA]. http://www.pria.com.au/priablog/revisiting-the-foundations-of-public-relations-education-in-australia

Gleeson, D. J. (2014). Public relations education in Australia, 1950–1975. *Journal of Communication Management, 18*, 193–206. doi:10.1108/JCOM-11-2012-0091.

Greenmount, L. (1990, February). The spotlight is focused on PR education courses. *Profile: The Newsletter of the Public Relations Institute of Australia (WA)*, p. 1.

Grunig, J., & Hunt, T. (1984). *Managing public relations.* New York, NY: Holt, Rinehart & Winston.

Hatherell, W., & Bartlett, J. (2006). Positioning public relations as an academic discipline in Australia. *Asia Pacific Public Relations Journal, 6*(2), 1–13.

International Public Relations Association [IPRA]. (1990, September). *Public relations education: Recommendations and standards* (Gold Paper No. 7). Report by the IPRA Education and Research Committee and the IPRA International Commission on Public Relations Education.

Johnston, J., & Macnamara, J. (2013). Public relations literature and scholarship in Australia: A brief history of change and diversification. *Prism, 10*(1). Retrieved from http://www.prismjournal.org/fileadmin/10_1/Johnston_Macnamara.pdf

Johnston, J., & Zawawi, C. (Eds.). (2000). *Public relations theory and practice.* St Leonards, Australia: Allen & Unwin.

June Dunstan takes on new WAIT PR course. (1986, February/March). *Profile: The Newsletter of the Public Relations Institute of Australia (WA),* p. 2.

Kerr, G. F., Waller, D., & Patti, C. (2009). Advertising education in Australia: Looking back to the future. *Journal of Marketing Education, 31,* 264–274. doi:10.1177/0273475309345001.

Kruckeberg, D. (1998). The future of PR education: Some recommendations. *Public Relations Review, 24*(2), 235–248. doi:10.1016/S0363-8111(99)80053-8.

L'Etang, J. (2004). *Public relations in Britain: A history of professional practice in the 20th century.* Mahwah, NJ: Lawrence Erlbaum.

L'Etang, J. (2009). "Radical PR"—Catalyst for change or an aporia? *Ethical Space: The International Journal of Communication Ethics, 6*(2), 13–18. Retrieved from http://www.communicationethics.net/journal/v6n2/v6n2_feat1.pdf

Lewis, G. (1982). The Anglo-American influence on Australian communication education. *Australian Journal of Communication, 1&2,* 14–20.

Macnamara, J. (1984). *Public relations handbook for managers and executives.* Melbourne, Australia: Margaret Gee Media.

Macnamara, J. (1992). *The Asia Pacific public relations handbook.* Lindfield, Australia: Archipelago Press.

Macnamara, J. (1996). *Public relations handbook for managers and executives* (Rev. ed.). Melbourne, Australia: Prentice Hall Australia.

Macnamara, J. (2000). *Jim Macnamara's public relations handbook.* Melbourne, Australia: Information Australia.

Maras, S. (2003). Presidents reflect on ANZCA: Past and future. *Australian Journal of Communication, 30*(1), 1–24.

Maras, S. (2004). Thinking about the history of ANZCA: An Australian perspective. *Australian Journal of Communication, 31*(2), 13–51.

Maras, S. (2006). The emergence of communication studies in Australia as "curriculum idea". *Australian Journal of Communication, 33*(2,3), 43–62.

Marginson, S., & Considine, M. (2000). *The enterprise university: Power, governance and reinvention in Australia*. Cambridge, England: Cambridge University Press.

Mathews, I. (1984). *How to use the media in Australia* (2nd ed.). Melbourne, Australia: Margaret Gee Media.

McKie, D. (2012). Textbook publishing: Opportunism, theory, and the captive audience. *Public Relations Inquiry, 1*, 107–110. doi:10.1177/20461 47X11422649.

Molloy, B., & Lennie, J. (1990). *Communication studies in Australia: A statistical study of teachers, students, and courses in Australian tertiary institutions* (Policy and research report No. 1). Brisbane, Australia: The Communication Centre, Queensland University of Technology.

Myers, H. (1976). Public relations and the future. In J. D. S. Potts (Ed.), *Public relations practice in Australia* (pp. 323–331). Sydney, Australia: McGraw-Hill.

National council accredits Western Australia's public relations course. (1984, December). *Profile: The Newsletter of the Public Relations Institute of Australia (WA)*, p. 1.

New breed of P.R. man. (1967, March/April). *Public Relations Journal*, p. 1.

NSW course in public relations. (1965, September/October). *Public Relations Journal*, p. 3.

Odd thoughts on PR. (1952, October). *Pro-Files*, p. 4.

Outline of the Mitchell College P.R. course. (1971, June/July). *Public Relations Australia*, pp. 10–11.

Patterson, H. E. (1952). New P.R. lecture course proposed [Letter to the editor]. *Pro-File, 1*(2), pp. 3–4.

Petelin, R. (2005). Editing from the edge: De-territorializing public relations scholarship. *Public Relations Review, 31*, 458–462. doi:10.1016/j.pubrev.2005.08.002.

Pieczka, M. (2002). Public relations expertise deconstructed. *Media Culture Society, 24*(3), 301–323. doi:10.1177/016344370202400302.

Pieczka, M. (2007). Case studies as narrative accounts of public relations practice. *Journal of Public Relations Research, 19*, 333–356. doi:10.1080/10627260701402432.

Plater, R. (1976). Public relations in Australia: Introduction by the National President of the Public Relations Institute of Australia. In J. D. S. Potts (Ed.), *Public relations practice in Australia* (p. iv). Sydney, Australia: McGraw Hill.

Potts, J. D. S. (Ed.). (1976). *Public relations practice in Australia*. Sydney, Australia: McGraw Hill.

Potts, J. D. S. (2008, November). *Evening with a Fellow*. Paper presented at the meeting of Public Relations Institute of Australia, Sydney, Australia. Retrieved from www.pria.com.au/resources//an-evening-with-a-fellow-david-potts-november-2008

PR industry at the crossroads: Results announced for first-ever survey of P.R. industry. (1985, October). *Profile: The Newsletter of the Public Relations Institute of Australia (WA)*, pp. 1–2.

PRIA (NSW) to run PR courses in Sydney. (1990, February). *Public Relations: An Official Journal of the Public Relations Institute of Australia (NSW)*, pp. 1–2.

Public relations course starts at WAIT in 1986. (1986, January). *Profile: The Newsletter of the Public Relations Institute of Australia (WA)*, p. 2.

Public relations education. (1966, March). *Public Relations Journal*, p. 21.

Public Relations Institute of Australia [PRIA]. (1991). *Guidelines for the accreditation of public relations courses at Australian tertiary institutions*. Sydney, Australia: Public Relations Institute of Australia.

Public Relations Institute of Australia [PRIA]. (1996). *Guidelines for the accreditation of public relations courses at Australian tertiary institutions*. Sydney, Australia: Public Relations Institute of Australia.

Public Relations Institute of Australia [PRIA]. (2012). David Potts FPRIA OAM recognized in Australia Day Honours List. Retrieved from http://www.pria. com.au/priablog/david-potts-fpria-oam-recognized-in-australia-day-honours-list

Putnis, P. (1986). Communication studies in Australia: Paradigms and contexts. *Media Culture Society, 8*, 143–157.

Putnis, P. (1988). The communication curriculum: Educating communication practitioners. *Australian Communication Review, 9*(2), 29–44.

Putnis, P., & Axford, B. (2002). Communication and media studies in Australian universities: Diverse, innovative and isomorphic. *Australian Journal of Communication, 29*(1), 1–20.

Quarles, J., & Potts, D. (1990, September). Public relations education in Australia: A report prepared for the National Executive of the Public Relations Institute of Australia. Sydney, Australia: Public Relations Institute of Australia.

Quarles, J., & Rowlings, B. (1993). *Practising public relations: A case study approach*. Melbourne, Australia: Longman Cheshire.

Raciti, M. (2010). Marketing Australian higher education at the turn of the 21st century: A précis of reforms, commercialisation and the new university hierarchy. *e-Journal of Business Education & Scholarship of Teaching, 4*(1), 32–41. Retrieved from http://www.ejbest.org/Volume4-Issue1.html

Ray, G. (1991, March). Public relations institute to accredit education programs. *Public Relations: Official Journal of the New South Wales and Victorian Branches of the Public Relations Institute of Australia*, pp. 1–2.

Report on education. (1990, October). *Public Relations: Official Journal of the New South Wales and Victorian Branches of the Public Relations Institute of Australia*, p. 4.

S.A. course in public relations. (1965, November/December). *Public Relations Journal*, p. 2.

Serle, G. (2000). Medley, Sir John Dudley Gibbs (Jack) (1891–1962). *Australian dictionary of biography*. Canberra, Australia: Australian National University. Retrieved from http://adb.anu.edu.au/biography/medley-sir-john-dudley-gibbs-jack-11101/text19763

Sherman, B., & Griffin, J. (1976). Public relations administration. In J. D. S. Potts (Ed.), *Public relations practice in Australia* (pp. 77–86). Sydney, Australia: McGraw Hill.

Starck, N. (1999). *Accredited or discredited? A qualitative study of public relations education at Australian universities*. Unpublished master's thesis, RMIT, Melbourne, Australia.

Student workshop gains wide industry support. (1989, October). *Profile: The Newsletter of the Public Relations Institute of Australia (WA)*, p. 2.

Top marks for state convention. (1989, October). *Profile: The Newsletter of the Public Relations Institute of Australia (WA)*, p. 1.

Top offers for top youngsters. (1989, October). *Profile: The Newsletter of the Public Relations Institute of Australia (WA)*, p. 2.

Training in S.A. (1967, March/April). *Public Relations Journal*, p. 7.

Tymson, C., & Sherman, B. (1987). *The Australian public relations manual*. Sydney, Australia: Millennium Books.

van Ruler, B. (2005). Professionals are from Venus, scholars are from Mars [Commentary]. *Public Relations Review, 31*, 159–173. doi:10.1016/j.pubrev.2005.02.022.

Walker, G. (1991, Spring). From the editor [Editorial]. *Public Relations Educators Association of Australia Newsletter*, p. 8.

Walkington, J., & Vanderheide, R. (2008, July 1–4). *Enhancing the pivotal roles in workplace learning and community engagement through transdisciplinary "cross talking."* Paper presented at the meeting of HERDSA International Conference: Engaging Communities, Rotorua, New Zealand. Retrieved from http://www.herdsa.org.au/wp-content/uploads/conference/2008/papers/Walkington.pdf

Weaver, C. K. (2016). Who's afraid of the big bad wolf? Critical public relations as a cure for media studies' fear of the dark. In J. L'Etang, D. McKie, N. Snow, & J. Xifra (Eds.), *The Routledge handbook of critical public relations* (pp. 260–273). Abingdon, England: Routledge.

Williams, M. (1996). Public relationship marketing. *The PRofessional: Issues on Communication, Corporate Affairs and Public Relations* [Special Issue: Marketing Communication], *1*(4), pp. 13–15.

Wright, D. (2011). History and development of public relations education in North America: A critical analysis. *Journal of Communication Management, 15*, 236–255. doi:10.1108/13632541111151005.

CHAPTER 3

Women, Feminization, and Professionalization

Abstract Women have worked in Australian public relations since before 1940, yet their historical contributions to the industry are seldom acknowledged. This chapter draws on archival and interview research to illustrate the ways women were involved in the post-World War II professionalization of public relations, which began with the establishment of professional institutes. The rapid feminization of public relations in the 1970s and 1980s contributed to increasing anxiety about the significance for its professional status and to renewed attempts to establish jurisdiction over public relations activity. Gender has thus played a significant but under-recognized role in the construction of public relation expertise. This chapter therefore investigates the problematic gendering of public relations, and recognizes women's contributions to the industry in Australia.

Keywords Australia • Feminization • Gender • History • Women • Public relations

© The Editor(s) (if applicable) and The Author(s) 2016
K. Fitch, *Professionalizing Public Relations*,
DOI 10.1057/978-1-137-57309-4_3

INTRODUCTION

This chapter investigates the gendering of public relations, focusing on women and public relations and the significance of the increasing number of women working in the industry. It analyses newspapers and industry archives and draws on interviews with senior PRIA members, practitioners, and educators regarding their public relations careers in order to understand gendered shifts in the nature of public relations work in the second half of the twentieth century. Widespread industry concerns in the 1980s and 1990s that a feminized workforce would devalue public relations work and therefore threaten its attempts to gain professional recognition were not evident in the journals and newsletters produced by state-based public relations institutes in the 1950s when women were still a minority in the industry. The increase in women working in public relations, an increase which began in the 1970s, contributed to a gendered stratification of public relations work. The expansion of Australian higher education offered opportunities for public relations to become established in universities, and resulted in a majority of female public relations graduates. However, anxiety around the number of (often university-educated) women, working in public relations contributed to the introduction of greater regulatory structures by the professional association. The coding of public relations as feminine continues to shape contemporary concerns in the industry. This chapter therefore investigates the relationship of women to public relations in the second half of the twentieth century in order to understand the significance of gender.

WOMEN, PUBLIC RELATIONS HISTORY AND HISTORIOGRAPHY

Public relations history, and particularly histories which attempt to assert public relations' professional status, are highly gendered in that women's historical contributions to public relations are seldom recognized and their contributions are often marginalized (Fitch, 2016a). But, understandings of public relations as a profession tend to elide gender; for example, Pieczka (2007)'s study of contemporary UK industry narratives concerning professional practice argued such accounts were significant for their genderlessness. The lack of critical perspectives marginalizes the role of women and, typically, professionalization marginalizes women's work (Davies, 1996; Witz, 1992). Despite increasing interest in public relations historiography there is a lack of "*her*storical perspective." (L'Etang, 2015, p. 355). As early as 1989, Creedon pointed to the "sketchy" history of women in public relations (1989, p. 26). Some US studies sought to rediscover women's contributions to the development of public relations (see, for example, Gower, 2001; Horsley, 2007; Lamme, 2001, 2007; Miller, 1997) and more recently UK and Australian scholars have explored women's experiences in public relations in the late twentieth century (see, for example, Fitch & Third, 2014; Yaxley, 2013) and the presence and role of women in the post-war period when professional institutes were established (L'Etang, 2015). In Australia, women were employed in public relations and related industries prior to World War II, sometimes in high-profile roles, and even served on state and national committees for industry bodies in the 1950s, but nevertheless women remain noticeably absent from Australian public relations history prior to the 1980s.

One recent publication, *Australian Women in Advertising in the Twentieth Century* (Dickenson 2016) offers a unique and evidence-based study of women working in advertising and related industries; indeed, it conceptualizes advertising broadly to include public relations, recognizing advertising agencies played a significant role in the development of public relations in Australia. Dickenson defines advertising as:

> the use of a specific set of skills in a range of paid and un-paid activities, including retail advertising, public relations, the creative industries, journalism, political activism and philanthropy, as well as mainstream advertising in order to promote products, services and ideas. (2016, pp. 13–14)

In fact such a definition could equally apply to public relations, with critical scholars arguing that most understandings of public relations are incorrectly limited to corporate and government communication activity (McKie & Munshi, 2007). The significance of expanding the understanding of what counts as public relations is that the kinds of activity that tend to be marginalized from mainstream and professional work—such as the "technical" and promotional aspects that are often associated with "women's work" or the highly feminized sectors such as fashion or event management—can be included.

As established in Chap. 1, Australian public relations history is generally constructed with reference to the post-World War II establishment of professional institutes, which emphasize the achievements of male founders and is strongly focused on its development towards professional recognition. Yet, there is evidence of women working in public relations and related fields such as advertising from the beginning of the twentieth century (Dickenson, 2016; Fitch, 2016b). For example, going outside professional association records, which in any case are patchy and at least in the early years, limited to a couple of state-based institutes, allows a broader understanding of public relations activity. To offer one example, the women-run Rachel Forster Hospital for Women and Children in Sydney relied on subscriptions and donations for its existence, and much of this work was conducted by voluntary committees for decades after its establishment early in the twentieth century. The hospital's first professional appeals officer was Beatrice Hoyles (Organiser for Rachel, 1940). Although Hoyles had not previously worked in a hospital, she had worked extensively overseas in media and promotional roles. Her experience included working in Paris in the records and casualty office for the London-based *Evening News* during World War I and as a partner in a shipping firm after the war. She then worked in the fashion industry in London before returning to France where she worked for an American publicity firm. Hoyles said the publicity firm's "system was the most perfect I have ever seen…the firm knew accurately what results it obtained from every advertisement inserted in continental newspapers." On returning to Australia, Hoyles worked in a publicity role for Denison manufacturing company in Australia and New Zealand, and then in Papua, where she was secretary to the managing director of the Steamship Trading Company and presented the early morning radio news. This account of Hoyle's work history offers a rich description of both global mobility and a diverse background relevant to public relations and promotional activity, including business and administrative skills gained across various sectors, an understanding of print, radio, and news organizations, and diverse publicity work. This history confirms that women had roles in public relations and related industries—acknowledging that the boundaries between sales, advertising, promotional, fundraising, and media work were permeable—prior to World War II.

Women's pathways into public relations were varied but often included voluntary work, or as in Hoyles's case, prior employment, often overseas in publicity, media-related, or business roles (Fitch, 2016b). Both these entry points suggest that class, or particular kinds of social and cultural capital, were significant if unacknowledged factors in obtaining public relations work. Prior to World War II, volunteering for social institutions such as churches, schools, and hospitals was common among middle-class women (Curthoys, 1975). In 1941, for instance, Mrs Norman Picot, an American, was appointed public relations officer at the Children's Hospital having worked in a voluntary capacity for the hospital's women's auxiliary for more than a decade; she had previously held an administrative position with the American Red Cross in New York during World War I (Public Relations Officer, 1941; Give It To A Busy Woman, 1943). Picot was responsible for the "maintenance and increase of the hospital's prestige in the public mind, publicity contacts with the Press and Radio, and co-operations with auxiliaries of the hospital." Retrospective biographies and contemporaneous newspaper articles from the 1940s and 1950s illustrate the global mobility of many successful female practitioners. As middle-class women were more likely to seek white collar employment, class remained a persistent contributor to suitability for the field. Dickenson drew similar conclusions regarding the significance of social position for women entering public relations and advertising, noting that they were primarily educated, middle-class women who travelled and "were previously extremely active on the social pages of newspapers" (2016, p. 71).

WOMEN AND PROFESSIONAL INSTITUTES

Women in the 1950s

An American study investigated the presence of women in a PRSA journal, in order to determine the level of acceptance of women by their male peers in the industry in the years 1945–1972 and gain a better understanding of women's contributions to the field. Gower found significant shifts in the representation of women, with "the decline in the presence of women in the *Journal* and their almost complete disappearance in 1958 and 1959" (2001, p. 17). In the late 1950s through to 1961, and in contrast to post-war years, the public relations industry was represented almost exclusively as a male profession, despite the fact that women increasingly entered public relations in the 1950s and, by 1960, made up one quarter of all practitioners. Although women initially were well represented in the US journal and positioned as contributors to the growing professionalism of the field in the decade following World War II, their presence in the journal later declined. It is difficult to compare the shifts in the representation of women Gower identified with the journals produced by the Australian public relations institutes, partly due to the lack of a national publication for many years but also because there was no single publication across the decades.

Despite the male-orientated "in honour" list offered by PRIA (see www.pria.com.au) and histories in textbooks, analysis of journals produced by two state institutes in the 1950s, PRIA (Vic)'s *Pro-Files* [1952–1958] and the Sydney-based AIPR's *P.R. News* [c. 1954–c. 1956], demonstrates both the presence of female practitioners and that they played roles in the establishment and management of the institutes, with women participating as council and committee members (Fitch, 2016b). The list of financial members for the Victorian institute in 1956 showed almost 15% (i.e., 14 out of 95) of members were women (That List, 1956). At least four of those women worked for John and Esta Handfield (Public Relations) Pty Ltd: Lee Keen, Nola Totham, Mary Wright, and of course Esta (New Members, 1956). Women identified in *Pro-Files* in the early and mid-1950s included foundation committee member of the Victorian institute, Bonnie McCallum, who was publicity officer at the Australian Broadcasting Commission from 1936 until her marriage in 1964 (McCallum, 1978); Emerald Goetze, public relations officer at the Victorian School for Deaf Children, who wrote feature articles in the journal; and 1955–1956 committee and editorial committee member Esta Handfield. Women identified in *P.R. News* in the mid-1950s include Phyllis (Phil) Parkinson, of Parkinson Publicity, who managed public relations for Australian National Wine Week, the national Annual Conference for the Australian Wine Board, and the Wine Information Centre for the Commonwealth; Lilian Roxon, a press relations officer for Sydney department store Anthony Horden & Sons, who spent four months studying retail stores in New York; Marj Sparrow, who worked at George Patterson Advertising; and Jessie Fawsitt, who worked for British Overseas Airways Corporation [BOAC]. Sparrow and Fawsitt were on AIPR's programme committee and assisted with the production of *P.R. News* by collaborating on a regular column; they were also institute fellows (Membership, 1955). A decade later, Fawsitt was the only female practitioner, out of 20 elected members, on the NSW state council, and this chapter discusses Fawsitt's public relations career below.

Global mobility allowed women to gain valuable experience for public relations work after the war, suggesting that a particular kind of social and cultural capital was necessary for an occupational fit (Edwards, 2014a, 2014b). Doreen Riley, for instance, had worked in England "with Baird Television Receivers, a job which put her on a television programme with the BBC, and took her to the continent to represent the firm, and to attend conferences" (Her Job is Public Relations, 1953). Riley described her work as a public relations consultant with Melbourne-based Aldwych

Advertising Pty Ltd as "not advertising" but rather "it is her responsibility to evolve ways and means of bringing clients for whom she acts as a
consultant in direct contact with the public. Industrial relations, personnel
relations, and so on come within her sphere" (Her Job is Public Relations,
1953). Riley also consulted for British Rubber Development Board, a
cooperative of rubber producers in Malaya and organized, along other
activities, the Dunlop Art Contest. Riley's comments illustrate attempts to
establish public relations as a unique service. As Riley's career trajectory
demonstrates, a background in media-related industries and media production offered relevant experience for public relations work. In addition
to not-for-profit, health, and manufacturing sectors, women found work
in public relations in retail, travel, and fashion sectors as part of the post-
war expansion of industrialization and manufacturing and, in tandem, the
growth in a consumer society in which public relations played a key role.

Disappearing Women in the 1960s and 1970s

In contrast to Gower's research on women in the PRSA journal, the
decline of women in Australian journals is notable much later than the
late 1950s. In part, this may be due to the fact that there was no ongoing
Australian journal produced by professional institutes in which shifts in
representation can be tracked, partly due to tensions between state-based
institutes and a federated body as well as financial pressures. Nevertheless,
analysing journals produced by Australian professional institutes in terms
of their "disciplining effect" in the construction of institutional norms
(Edwards & Pieczka, 2013, p. 20) reveals an increased marginalization
of women in public relations by the late 1960s and early 1970s in comparison with the state-institute-produced journals of the 1950s (where
women were in the minority in any case). Whole issues in this later period
exist without a single reference to the existence of women. Only a hand-
ful of articles in *Public Relations Journal* and *Public Relations Australia*
between 1965 and 1972 were written by women, including a book review
in 1970, where the author foregrounded her "novice" status (McIndoe,
1970). Most job advertisements throughout these years use the male pro-
noun, with only two advertisements specifying the position is available for
"male or female" applicants (Editor, male or female, 1969; Hydro-electric
Commission, 1968).

This lack of representation of female practitioners in journals, conferences, and state institute committees does not reflect membership levels.

In 1970, women made up one quarter of the reported new, regraded and resigned members in Victoria (Vic. Membership, 1970), yet are poorly represented in the journal pages. In 1968, 56 of the 480 (i.e., 11.7%) of institute members were women. Just over half of the female members held professional-grade memberships where they were entitled to use the nominals APRIA, MPRIA or FPRIA (PRIA Membership List, 1968). Twenty-six of the 56 women, as either affiliates or student members, were non-professional grade members. Most of the 17 Fellows, the elite, invitation-only membership category, were male consultants who had been associated with establishing state institutes in the 1950s. Despite a tenfold increase in membership of the professional institute, and similar levels of overall female membership with the 1950s, women appear to be systematically excluded or marginalized from the cognitive, normative, and symbolic mechanisms of professionalization identified by Noordegraaf (2011) and over-represented in the non-professional membership grades.

A compelling example of the systematic exclusion of women from institutional structures is found in the reports of annual state and national council elections. In contrast to the early years of the state-based institute, there is a near total absence of women on state councils. For example, in 1970/1971, the state councils of NSW, South Australia, Victoria, and the newly formed Western Australian institute had no female members (New W.A. Chapter, 1971). The state of Tasmania, where Penny Cresswell played a prominent role as interstate liaison officer, and office bearers included three female members in 1970 and four in 1971 (Tasmanian Secretary, 1969; New Tas. Council, 1970), was a notable exception. Cresswell also served as Tasmanian delegate to the National Council (Tasmanian Secretary, 1969) and was the sole female member of the organizing committee for the 3rd National Public Relations Convention in April 1969 in Sydney (National Convention, 1968); Cresswell can be seen in an illustrated cover as the single woman in a room full of men as members of the national council (Cover Design, 1968). In contrast to the Western Australian public relations institute, Clara Behrend was the first female president of the Western Australian Division of the Australian Advertising Institute of Australia in 1954, a position she held for 18 years with an entirely male committee throughout this time; her work covered retail advertising, sales promotion, and public relations, and she was elected a Fellow of the Advertising Association of Australia in 1936 (Dickenson, 2016). While Behrend and Cresswell may have been exceptions, Behrend's longstanding presidency demonstrates that public relations institutes did not have complete jurisdiction over public relations activity and that women did achieve and indeed maintain significant leadership roles outside of those institutes.

Women were also poorly represented as "expert" speakers and presenters at the four-day national conventions in 1969 and 1971, which featured 64 and 34 speakers respectively; none were women, although Penny Cresswell was the guest speaker at the informal dinner dance to close the 1971 conference (Third National Public Relations, 1969; Programme, 1971). The 1966 four-day convention included one woman out of a total of 21 speakers; Esta Handfield chaired a session on "Graphic Arts in Communications" (Public Relations in a Shrinking World, 1966). Female practitioners are occasionally acknowledged in announcements of new appointments and industry moves. Often, these new appointees would look after women's interest accounts, highlighting that opportunities for women in the industry in particular sectors or fields were highly gendered. Pauline McGrath, for example, established her own company Etcetera, after managing women's interest accounts for Esta and John Handfield's Image Australia, and then spent two years in London working for Lonsdale Hands Organisation, before returning to Australia to manage the Handfields' Sydney office (New Appointments, 1968; Etcetera, 1969). Echoing Gower's (2001) observations regarding lower barriers to entry into public relations work, Handfield later wrote of McGrath's career, from her initial recruitment as:

> a fresh-faced 16-year-old who answered an advertisement for an office junior … Perhaps because a public relations consultant's office is a little more open than the traditional business, she was able to use her talents and quickly moved from clerical to public relations work. (1976a, p. 53)

However, female practitioners did not only work on women's interest accounts, as a 1968 membership list confirms women worked for trade associations and in manufacturing, hospitality, not-for-profit, government, and consultancy sectors (PRIA Membership List, 1968). Olive Kellie, for example, was a senior consultant specializing "in public relations and publicity associated with machinery, engineering and construction projects" and "had conducted campaigns for grout concrete additives, industrial felt and refrigeration controls" (Appointments, 1968).

WOMEN AND PUBLIC RELATIONS WORK

Fashioning Careers

Jessie Fawsitt's Australian public relations career spanned several decades. Fawsitt, a qualified pilot, but variously described as "an attractive young English publicity officer" and "a former London typist," was a BOAC public relations officer, having previously worked for the same organization in London (Arrived on a Visit, 1949; Airline Girl, 1953). Initially Fawsitt was responsible for "interviewing agents, arranging window displays, dealing with press publicity and occasional secretarial work for executives visiting from overseas" (Arrived on a Visit, 1949), but by the early 1950s her main responsibility was to interest women in air travel and much of her work involved fashion and travel, compering fashion parades throughout Australia and New Zealand, and doing numerous press and promotional tours for the airline. Fawsitt worked with "many media—the press, radio, films, exhibitions, window displays, posters, photographs and colourful literature" and she extended her role by "compering fashion parades of clothes suitable for air travel" (Air News, 1954). One of her more creative ideas was to commission an all-climate wardrobe within the 66lb luggage limit for international flights, and travel around the world (All-climate Wardrobe, 1954; Fashion Flight, 1954; Her Job Is Air Travel, 1954). The wardrobe, comprising primarily Australian-made nylon and silk garments, was supplied by Melbourne-based House of Leroy. Destinations included Honolulu, London, Lisbon, Madrid, Paris, Rome, Beirut, Karachi, Rangoon, Bangkok and Singapore. Fawsitt modelled the clothes at exotic locations and promoted Australian fashion to the world through television and press interviews. Fawsitt's world tour received extensive coverage in the Australian media, and she toured Australia on her return, wrote articles offering travel and fashion advice, and gave demonstrations on the art of packing (Fawsitt, 1954a, 1954b, 1954c; Traveller To Display, 1954). Fawsitt's presentations were promoted through extensive media campaigns and paid advertising:

> Miss Fawsitt, travel advisor for British Overseas Airways Corporations, will present her All-Australian, round-the-world, Leroy wardrobe, designed to provide style and variety, for every occasion from sightseeing to cocktails. You are invited to listen to her sparkling commentary, whilst mannequins parade for your interest these up-to-the-minute Leroy Fashions. (Leroy-BOAC World Fashion Paradettes, 1954)

Fawsitt completed another round-the-world trip in 1959, this time show-casing Australian wool garments supplied by the department store, David Jones. Colour features, showing the garments being modelled by local actors and models in exotic locations—such as Wat Po temple in Bangkok, the Temple of Jupiter near Beirut, on the Champs Elysees in Paris, Fisherman's Wharf in San Francisco, a beach in Honolulu, and in front of the Houses of Parliament in London—were included in Australian wom-en's magazines and in local and international press (Wool Wings Its Way, 1959). On her return, Fawsitt again travelled throughout Australia with a hectic schedule of twice- or even thrice-daily department store visits giving "how-to-pack" demonstrations and discussing her recent round the world trip (Weekly Round, 1959).

Fawsitt's professional activity, outlined in her industry news column, included organizing and compering beauty pageants, fashion parades, and photography exhibitions in Australia and New Zealand, managing rela-tionships with department stores, and ensuring extensive media cover-age (What We're Doing, 1956). Fawsitt was on the state committee for PRIA (Vic) in the 1950s and 1960s where she worked on programming and editorial subcommittees and by 1955 was awarded the Honour of Fellow. Fawsitt had various job titles in media coverage including Press and Display Officer (Air News, 1954; Airline Girl, 1953; Talkabout, 1954); Publicity Officer (Interesting People, 1948); and Public Relations Officer (All-climate Wardrobe, 1954), suggesting the terms were inter-changeable. By the end of the decade, her role was more often reported as BOAC's "travel consultant" or even "women's travel advisor" (Weekly Round, 1959). Fawsitt's public relations career illustrates opportunities for women in the post-war era of increasing industrialization and con-sumption, and the growing interest in marketing specifically to women.

Negotiating Professional Identities

Esta Handfield, formerly Esther O'Donnell, was well known in the Victorian public relations industry. Esta Handfield, later the first female president of Victorian institute, came to public relations through a brief stint in radio and advertising, working with the Department of Post War Reconstruction, O'Brien Publicity in Melbourne, and Mather & Crowther, the English advertising agency that would much later become Ogilvy & Mather, in London (Speakers, 1966). She was elected a full member of the Victorian institute in 1953 (eligibility was one year's fulltime work in a public relations role) (Personal, 1953). Together with her husband John, whom she married in 1949, Esta managed a public relations consultancy. Initially, it was known as Metro Publicity Services, but from 1952 the Handfields consulted under their own names because "of the confusion that was being caused by different interpretations of the word 'publicity'" (Personal, 1952). The consultancy was renamed Image Australia in the 1960s and, according to one advertisement, had offices in Melbourne, Sydney, Adelaide, Brisbane, Perth, and London as well as associates in Auckland and Manila (Image Australia, 1966). In 2002 at a 50th anniversary dinner of the Victorian institute, John Flower stated "Today's term for Esta, without doubt, would be feisty"; he noted her "fierce independence" and that the Handfield's consultancy was one of the first in Melbourne: "they were a remarkable couple, and tough ... politically savvy and robust."[1] Dennis Rutzou (2010), who began his public relations career working for the Handfields in October 1957, stated that he then referred to public relations practitioners as "the gin and tonic men," noting that Esta was one of "very few females in PR in those days."

The Handfields' professional activity ranged from the end of the 1940s and lasted until the 1980s. Their consultancy produced annual reports, celebratory books such as *Moorabbin: A Centenary History 1862–1962*; exhibition programmes such as *One World of Fashion* (1959) for an international trade fair; as well as managing women's interest accounts, corporate campaigns, and social advocacy work. Image Australia established Steel Can People in 1971 to promote the national recycling of steel cans; the scheme was funded by BHP and steel can makers J Gadsen Aus Ltd and Containers Ltd and Esta Handfield was the public relations officer for the scheme, which critics alleged to be a front group. (Madden 1973). Their work and clients were diverse. Esta Handfield co-developed and produced a film for the Australian Women's Surfriders Association (1986), *Women in the Surf*, which was partly funded by the Women's Film Fund of the Australian Film Commission, the Victorian Department of Sport and Recreation; and Europe Strength Food Company.

Esta Handfield was a member of the editorial panel and the features editor for *Pro-Files* in 1956 and later became president of PRIA (Vic). She was the only woman on the programming committee for the 1964 national convention, and, with Don Barnes, collated and edited the conference proceedings (PRIA, 1964). Handfield was one of only two women to write a chapter in Dwyer's (1961) book. In that chapter, "The Methods of Public Relations," Handfield positions public relations as "an organized professional activity" that developed out of technological change and through education, demanding prestige and detachment, and argued that public relations must act as "the conscience of management" (1961, p. 15, 22).

Handfield (1976a) wrote a book, *Double Bed and Separate Bank Account*, "to help women navigate the different dimensions of their lives with family, home and career." The book is testament to 1970s' second wave feminism, and includes practical advice for returning to the workforce after having children and running the household (including shopping and cooking tips), and offers career development advice. Handfield acknowledges on the cover she is a PRIA Fellow and a former state president, and refers in the book to her public speaking engagements as a member of "the speaker's panel for the Public Relations Institute" (1976a, p. 28). Handfield promoted her book through a media campaign and workshops for women (see Handfield, 1974, 1976b). In one chapter, "Identi-dress," Handfield offers fashion advice to assist working women in navigating their professional identity and Handfield's observations echo Demetrious's recognition nearly four decades later of "fashion as grammar or rules which direct the development of professional identities" (2014, p. 23). For Demetrious, analysis of "the clothes-body complex" offers powerful understandings of the creation and construction of meanings on gendered roles in public relations and the ongoing tension between professionalism and sexualization (2014, p. 26, 33). Given Demetrious's positioning of the significance of dress, and Haynes's (2012) identification of a close link with between professional identity and gendered embodiment in masculine professions, Handfield's comments on fashion are insightful. She opens the chapter by discussing a speech on fashion she was invited to give to professional women. Handfield suggested her audience, high achieving, drably dressed women in their late 50s, demonstrated their career and professional success through their conventional dress and lack of personal style, which Handfield attributed to their desire "to be accepted as women," despite their professional achievements (1976a, p. 29). Handfield offers guidelines to working women in "dressing effectively" to establish their executive status:

> Fur and leather have a lot to offer the business woman. ... Furs, particularly, separate the women from the girls. Wear an expensive exciting fur or a luxurious leather coat and nobody is going to take you for a stenographer. (1976a, p. 30)

For Handfield, "effective dressing" embraces both business and sexual identities, and significantly for the development of the public relations occupational identity, Handfield identifies the need to ensure that women are not mistaken as stenographers, secretaries, or office workers but rather claim power through their fashion choices.

Bumping the Glass Ceiling

Women working in public relations in the 1980s were usually university educated, although this qualification was often in any discipline rather than a communication studies, business, or public relations degree. Further, experience of travel and work overseas continued to ease pathways into the industry. Although women still entered public relations through secretarial and stenography roles, this appeared to be rarer (Fitch & Third, 2014). In interviews, university-educated women often described the start of their career in public relations as accidental. For example, Wendy Yorke gained a Bachelor of Arts (Philosophy) in England in 1981 and was employed in the publications department at Sotheby's before working first in Hong Kong and then travelling to Australia. She arrived in Sydney where she met the director of Sydney's then-new Powerhouse Museum, who offered her the temporary role of Head of Public Relations to cover maternity leave in 1983. In Yorke's words: "I had no experience in managing people or government administration but I said yes, being the sort of confident young English traveller and then of course I really got into it." Yorke attributed her entry into public relations as a combination of "good for-tune" and her "extrovert personality." She described her museum work primarily as community relations, involving "writing media statements and entertaining media and then also taking photographs and getting articles in magazines and promoting the Powerhouse before it had opened" and later "running launches of exhibitions." In 1984, Yorke moved to Perth, where she worked for the multinational Australian consultancy Eric White Associates (EWA). However, Yorke found it difficult as both a woman and an outsider, recognizing the significance of existing professional networks: "I think [male boss] resented me because I was not an ex-journo and in those days in Perth PR was all about media exposure and to be a PR expert you were expected to be an ex-*West Australian* [newspaper] journo ... the local boys club!" Yorke joined PRIA precisely because "the state members of the PRIA were definitely working to make it a more professional career path and a better recognized part of the corporate business" (Welcome to

Eight, 1984). Yorke was employed by one of EWA's major clients in the agricultural sector; she was their first public relations officer. Yorke maintains she was never discriminated against yet describes a gendered hierarchy in public relations work and recounts how male managers were appointed over her to focus on media relations while she was responsible for community and internal relations. Yorke's duties included organizing a staff party, managing an internal staff survey, writing a regular newsletter, managing corporate events, and introducing a new logo and branding. However, "the sort of more serious stuff—i.e., the media management ...well [male boss] did." The boys' network of former journalists continued to impact the corporate world: "they maintained this old boy network within their corporate positions, and that's where women found it very hard to break in." A keen sailor, Yorke left in 1986 to work for renowned advertising agency—then the largest in Australia—Mojo, who were establishing a public relations office in Perth, MoJo Corporate, to manage Bond Brewing's A$15 million sponsorship commitments with the Australian 1986–1987 defence of the America's Cup (Mojo Corporate Opens, 1986). The yacht race attracted significant commercial and government investment in Perth. In Yorke's words, she was always "much better at the stakeholder and relationship building areas of public relations" and

> the marketing and the advertising and the publicity and PR took on an almost playful kind of aspect for that year when there was a lot of money around and everyone jumped on that bandwagon and I think that opened the door for people like ... myself to do really well.

Yorke's role included managing Swan Brewery's extensive sponsorship commitments, promoting the launch of Ken Done's Black Swan Art Gallery and clothing range as well as restaurant launches, and managing the National Enterprise Conference. Female interview participants identified the 1980s as "opening up" new opportunities for women in public relations and more broadly in terms of public relations work (Fitch & Third, 2014). Yorke identifies 1986 as the point at which public relations, at least in Perth, began to be understood as something more than simply media relations:

> Rather than being just about media relations and customers' newsletters, it [public relations] was expanding hugely and companies were suddenly seeing the value of other aspects, putting credit in the bank so to speak and

forming strategic alliances and better relations with customers and others for improved business functions and I think the growth of public relations made it possible for corporations to be much more open and honest about what they were doing.

After the America's Cup in early 1987, Yorke followed her husband to Hong Kong, where she established her own public relations consultancy; in fact, many women left corporate work to establish consultancies in the 1980s and found that the consultancy sector offered more diverse and challenging work and greater autonomy outside highly gendered corporate hierarchies (Fitch & Third, 2014).

GENDER AND EDUCATION

Women, Public Relations, and Education

As Yorke observed, public relations was a highly gendered industry in Australia in the 1980s, partly due to the number of male ex-journalists working in public relations roles. Research conducted in 1985 found that journalism was a common route for men, but not women, into public relations roles; although almost half (46%) of the participants in that study had backgrounds in journalism, fewer women (only 28% of female participants) had entered the industry via journalism (PR Industry, 1985). Interview participants described public relations in the 1980s and even in the 1990s as "very blokey" (Fitch & Third, 2014). The significance of this gendering for public relations is an increasingly segregated industry, with implications for how professional activity, expertise, and knowledge in public relations are constituted. B. Mackey, who served as a state and national PRIA president in the 1980s, confirmed Yorke's experiences and similarly described what was effectively a "boys' network" that assisted practitioners in obtaining media coverage, and maintained that in the 1980s, public relations relied on relationships between journalists and ex-journalists. He observed: "Practically every one of them [public relations practitioners] had joined the newspaper from school as a cadet … and they were all convinced the only people who could do [public relations] were ex-journalists because that's where we all come from." Other participants observed in the 1970s and 1980s that public relations expertise was understood primarily as the capacity to network with journalists. Yet, for Yorke, 1986 was a significant turning point in that public relations began to be understood more broadly as stakeholder and relationship management.

PRIA's professionalization agenda in the 1980s contributed to changing industry attitudes towards university education. B. Mackey acknowledged that although few of the practitioners who were former journalists had studied at university, the industry began to value a broad university education, as graduates "actually knew about the constitution ... political history in this country and ... about social welfare." Initially, the particular qualification was not significant. In 1989, for instance, the Perth office of International Public Relations announced the appointment of three new consultants: all women and all university graduates (New Faces at IPR, 1989). Their qualifications included a Bachelor of Science (Psychology and Human Physical Performance); a Bachelor of Arts (English and Comparative Literature); and a Bachelor of Arts (Journalism and Business).

The introduction of public relations courses to higher education contributed to the increasing feminization of the industry, with estimates of the proportion of women working in public relations increasing from 10% in the early 1970s to approximately 50% in the early 1980s (Zawawi, 2009). In 1989, women made up 42% (90 of 214) financial members of the public relations institute in Western Australia.[2] In 2002, Rea noted that "women are pouring ... into higher education courses in public relations" in Australia and dominated public relations teaching, and that as a result of its "steady feminisation" in Australia in previous decades the "face of public relations is female" (2002, p. 1, 2). Certainly, the numerical dominance of female students in public relations courses into the 1990s is confirmed in a number of sources, including the Quarles and Potts (1990) report, which claimed women made up 80% of public relations students at Australian universities. A 1997 national study, partially funded by PRIA's NEC, investigated the attitudes of 82 graduates of PRIA-accredited degrees towards their education; 87% of participants were female (PR Education, 1997). Similarly, Rea (2002) suggests anecdotal evidence confirms female students made up approximately 80% of Australian public relations courses.

Feminization and Professionalization

Although PRIA welcomed the introduction of public relations as a university-level course of study, the institute was less enthusiastic about the number of women, often university educated, entering the industry (Fitch & Third, 2014). One interview participant acknowledged "professions that are dominated by women, like nursing and teaching, are the ones where salaries don't increase as much as they should" and that public relations was in danger of being relegated to a support or technical function rather than a profession (Participant 9). The issue of the industry's feminization was an ongoing concern for PRIA in the 1980s and into the 1990s, with a perceived need to guard against public relations being thought of as a "pink profession" (Participant 9) as public relations "would devalue" and "be downgraded" (Participant 10). Such perceptions are supported by the findings of the PRIA-commissioned ChanMac Services report in 1985, discussed in Chap. 1, which found that Australian public relations practitioners were paid less than other professionals in the same organizations, and there were significant discrepancies in salaries along gendered lines (PR Industry, 1985). Tymson, a former PRIA state and national president, described how these concerns dominated discussions at the PRIA (NSW) state council in the 1980s and that the high proportion of female graduates was perceived as "a major industry problem." The industry response to the growing feminization of public relations was to develop greater regulation of professional structures designed to demarcate professional public relations from non-professional activity and ensure greater exclusivity among its membership (Fitch & Third, 2014). Significant stratification emerged along gendered lines between technical (non-professional) and strategic or professional activities in public relations, and across different sectors (Fitch & Third, 2010, 2014). Women, for example, were more likely to enter public relations through promotional activity and from not-for-profit and marketing sectors than from journalism (Fitch & Third, 2014). Despite the increase in the number of women working in public relations, women were more likely to remain in certain sectors such as community relations and not-for-profit and in low level, technical roles such as marketing and promotion; women were often excluded from more strategic public relations activity and found it difficult to advance within corporate structures, despite being more likely to be university educated than their male colleagues.

The significance for this book is the industry's ambivalent attitude towards higher education. On the one hand, university education was perceived to enhance the professional standing of public relations and reposition it as a management discipline. On the other hand, participants identify the introduction of university-level public relations courses resulted in large numbers of female public relations graduates, posing a threat to the professional standing of the field. University education therefore was perceived by participants to play a pivotal role in both the positive outcome of developing professional standards, but also, less favourably, in the feminization of the public relations industry. The increasing regulation of PRIA membership, an important part of maintaining a jurisdiction over the industry, can therefore also be seen in part as a response to the professional anxiety evoked by the rapid feminization of the field (Fitch & Third, 2010, 2014). Yet, paradoxically, women were experiencing successful careers (as in fact they have throughout the history of public relations in Australia) and contributed to, and indeed supported, PRIA's professionalization agenda.

Women and Professionalization

Women have always worked in public relations in Australia, and did not suddenly appear when the industry underwent rapid feminization in the 1980s. Although this chapter focused on the second half of the twentieth century, women worked in public relations roles prior to World War II, and, if we adopt a broad understanding of public relations activity, women were widely employed across advertising, marketing, and media work. Global mobility was significant for all the women discussed in this chapter: from Hoyles prior to World War II, to Fawsitt and Yorke who both came from England to Australia, albeit four decades apart, and both Handfield and McGrath worked in advertising and marketing agencies in London early in their careers. These factors suggest that class was indeed an informal credential for women's entry into public relations. Many of the women who worked in Australian public relations had lived and worked abroad, often in England, as this was a typical pattern for middle-class Australians. Further, as Dickenson (2016) noted in relation to women in advertising, colonial networks were significant in the development of both the public relations industry and opportunities for women to gain relevant experience for public relations work in Australia.

Although in the minority in the fledgling professional institutes, women nevertheless participated in the early mechanisms of professionalization in the 1950s: they contributed to journals and participated on state councils and state institute programming and editorial committees. In contrast, in the late 1960s and early 1970s, women appeared to be increasingly marginalized from institutional structures, despite the fact that the ratio of women to men among institute members had not changed significantly. With the exception of Tasmania, there were no women on state institute councils in 1970/1971. There were very few feature articles by women in the *Public Relations Journal* and *Public Relations Australia* [1965–1972], and women were represented primarily as wives, secretaries, or as novice, rather than as expert, practitioners.

In part, this may be due to the dominance of former journalists working in public relations in the 1970s and the emphasis on media relations and social and cultural capital gained through those networks. The "boys' club" mentality translated into corporate spheres as male journalists became more established in the corporate world, where they continued to rely on their old networks. But the public relations workforce changed in response to broader societal changes concerning women and work. The introduction of public relations as a university course of study, and its significant growth throughout the 1980s, contributed to and accelerated the feminization of public relations. This shift led to renewed attempts by the industry to gain professional recognition, in part through establishing greater regulation of, and jurisdiction over, public relations. Exploring the historical contributions of women to public relations demonstrates the impact of gender on the Australian industry, particularly in terms of its professionalization, as well as develops an important, yet neglected, aspect of public relations history. The inclusion of women in public relations histories highlights the gendered construction of professional expertise and occupational identity, evident in the growing exclusion of women from representation in professional institutes and in particular kinds of public relations work. It also highlights the significance of other factors such as class and global mobility that contributed to pathways into, and careers in, public relations in the post-war period.

NOTES

1. Flower, J. (2002, August 15). 50th Anniversary Dinner [Text of speech]. Letter dated 16 December 2002 to Mark Sheehan. Photocopy in possession of author.
2. PRIA (WA) financial members at 30 June 1989. (1989, July). [Supplement]. *Profile: The Newsletter of the Public Relations Institute of Australia (WA)*, n.p.

REFERENCES

Air news. (1954, August 19). *Balonne Beacon*, p. 5.
Airline girl will beat race planes. (1953, October 1). *The Newcastle Sun*, p. 18.

All-climate wardrobe weighs only 66lb. (1954, February 19). *The Newcastle Sun*, p. 10.

Appointments. (1968, November/December). *Public Relations Australia*, p. 11.

Arrived on a visit, decided to stay. (1949, July 16). *News*, p. 11.

Cover design. (1968, June/July). *Public Relations Australia*, p. 3.

Creedon, P. J. (1989). Public relations history misses "her story." *Journalism Educator, 44*(3), 26–30.

Curthoys, A. (1975). Towards a feminist labour history. In A. Curthoys, S. Eade, & P. Spearritt (Eds.), *Women at work* (pp. 88–95). Canberra, Australia: Australian Society for the Study of Labour History.

Davies, C. (1996). The sociology of professions and the profession of gender. *Sociology, 30*, 661–678. doi:10.1177/0038038596030004003.

Demetrious, K. (2014). Surface effects: Public relations and the politics of gender. In C. Daymon & K. Demetrious (Eds.), *Gender and public relations: Critical perspectives on voice, image and identity* (pp. 20–45). Abingdon, UK: Routledge.

Dickenson, J. (2016). *Australian women in advertising in the twentieth century*. Houndmills, UK: Palgrave Macmillan.

Dwyer, T. (Ed.). (1961). *The Australian public relations handbook*. Melbourne, Australia: Ruskin.

Editor, male or female. (1969, March/April). [Advertisement]. *Public Relations Australia*, p. 13.

Edwards, L. (2014a). Discourse, credentialism and occupational closure in the communications industries: The case of public relations in the UK. *European Journal of Communication, 29*, 319–334. doi:10.1177/0267323113519228.

Edwards, L. (2014b). *Power, diversity and public relations*. London, UK: Routledge.

Edwards, L., & Pieczka, M. (2013). Public relations and "its" media: Exploring the role of trade media in the enactment of public relations' professional project. *Public Relations Inquiry, 2*(1), 5–25. doi:10.1177/2046147X12 464204.

Etcetera. (1969, July/August). *Public Relations Australia*, p. 7.

Fashion flight round the world. (1954, February 25). *The Sydney Morning Herald*, p. 4.

Fawsitt, J. (1954a, September 27). Expert's golden rules. *Sydney Morning Herald*, p. 3.

Fawsitt, J. (1954b, November 20). Hints and tips for travellers by air. *Queensland Times*, p. 3.

Fawsitt, J. (1954c, December 3). Complete wardrobe for a round-world air tour: Hints and tips for travellers. *Nambour Chronicle and North Coast Advertiser*, p. 3.

Fitch, K. (2016). Feminism and public relations. In J. L'Etang, D. McKie, N. Snow, & J. Xifra (Eds.), *Routledge handbook of critical public relations* (pp. 54–64). London, UK: Routledge.

Fitch, K., & Third, A. (2010). Working girls: Revisiting the gendering of public relations. *Prism, 7*(4). Retrieved from http://www.prismjournal.org/fileadmin/Praxis/Files/Gender/Fitch_Third.pdf

Fitch, K., & Third, A. (2014). Ex-journos and promo girls: Feminization and professionalization in the Australian public relations industry. In C. Daymon & K. Demetrious (Eds.), *Gender and public relations: Critical perspectives on voice, image and identity* (pp. 247–267). Abingdon, England: Routledge.

Give it to a busy woman. (1943, November 27). *The Age*, p. 8.

Gower, K. (2001). Rediscovering women in public relations: Women in the Public Relations Journal, 1945–1972. *Journalism History, 27*(1), 14–21.

Handfield, E. (1974, October 30). Double bed and separate bank accounts. *The Australian Women's Weekly*, pp. 35, 37.

Handfield, E. (1976a). *Double bed and separate bank account*. Carlton, Australia: Platypus Press.

Handfield, E. (1976b, May 19). Are you ready to return to the workforce? A positive guide for women. *The Australian Women's Weekly*, pp. 30–31.

Haynes, K. (2012). Body beautiful? Gender, identity and the body in professional services firms. *Gender, Work & Organization, 19*, 489–507. doi:10.1111/j.1468-0432.2011.00583.x.

Her job is air travel. (1954, September 8). *The Advertiser*, p. 20.

Her job is public relations. (1953, May 22). *The Advertiser*, p. 11.

Horsley, J. (2009). Women's contributions to American public relations, 1940–1970. *Journal of Communication Management, 13*, 100–115. doi:10.1108/13632540910951731.

Hydro-electric commission, Tasmania, has a vacancy for a publicity officer. (1968, February/March). [Advertisement]. *Public Relations Australia*, p. 19.

Image Australia. (1966, October/November). [Advertisement]. *Public Relations Journal*, p. 16.

Interesting people. (1948, July 3). *The Australian Women's Weekly*, p. 10.

Lamme, M. O. (2001). Furious desires and victorious careers: Doris E. Fleischman, counsel on public relations and advocate for working women. *American Journalism, 18*(3), 13–33. doi:10.1080/08821127.2001.10739322.

Lamme, M. O. (2007). Outside the prickly nest: Revisiting Doris Fleischman. *American Journalism, 24*(3), 85–107. doi:10.1080/08821127.2007.10678080.

L'Etang, J. (2015). "It's always been a sexless trade"; "It's clean work"; "There's very little velvet curtain": Gender and public relations in post-Second World War Britain. *Journal of Communication Management, 19*(4), 354–370. doi:10.1108/JCOM-01-2014-0006.

Madden, J. (1973, July 11). The can people—BHP can fraud detailed. *Woroni*, pp. 4–12.

McCallum, B. (1978). *Tales untold: Memoirs of an ABC publicity officer*. Melbourne, Australia: Hawthorn Press.

McIndoe, L. (1970, February/March). Communication is easy, or is it? *Public Relations Australia*, p. 11.

McKie, D., & Munshi, D. (2007). *Reconfiguring public relations: Ecology, equity and enterprise*. Abingdon, England: Routledge.

Membership. (1955, November–December). *P.R. News*, pp. 12–15.

Miller, K. S. (1997). Woman, man, lady, horse: Jane Stewart, public relations executive. *Public Relations Review, 23*, 249–269. doi:10.1016/S0363-8111(97)90035-7.

Mojo Corporate opens in Perth. (1986, July). *Campaign Brief* [page unknown].

National convention in Sydney next April. (1968, April/May). *Public Relations Australia*, p. 1.

New appointments. (1968, February/March). *Public Relations Australia*, p. 7.

New faces at IPR. (1989, September). *Profile: The Newsletter of the Public Relations Institute of Australia (WA)*, p. 3.

New members. (1956, July). *Pro-Files, 4*(2), p. 5.

New Tas. council. (1970, November/December). *Public Relations Australia*, p. 7.

New W.A. chapter. (1971, January/February). *Public Relations Australia*, p. 3.

Noordegraaf, M. (2011). Remaking professionals? How associations and professional education connect professionalism and organizations. *Current Sociology, 59*, 465–488. doi:10.1177/0011392111402716.

One world of fashion. (1959). [Programme, International Trade Fair, Exhibition Building, Melbourne, 26 February–14 March]. Melbourne, Australia: John and Esta Handfield (Public Relations).

Organiser for Rachel Forster Hospital: Miss B. Hoyles appointed. (1940, July 18). *Sydney Morning Herald*, p. 14.

Personal. (1952). *Pro-Files, 1*(3), p. 6.

Personal. (1953, March). *Pro-Files, 1*(5), p. 5.

Pieczka, M. (2007). Case studies as narrative accounts of public relations practice. *Journal of Public Relations Research, 19*, 333–356. doi:10.1080/10627260701402432.

PR education: Graduate perceptions. (1997, May). *Profile*, p. 5.

PR industry at the crossroads: Results announced for first-ever survey of P.R. industry. (1985, October). *Profile: The Newsletter of the Public Relations Institute of Australia (WA)*, pp. 1–2.

PRIA membership list. (1968, April/May). *Public Relations Australia* [Supplement], pp. i–xii.

Programme, Public Relations National Convention. (1971, August/September). *Public Relations Australia* [Supplement between pp. 6–7].

Public relations in a shrinking world. (1966, March). [Conference program]. *Public Relations Journal*, pp. 18–19.

Public Relations Institute of Australia [PRIA]. (1964). *Public relations in a changing world by Don Barnes, Esta Handfield*. Conference proceedings, National Convention of Public Relations Institute of Australia, Sydney, Australia.

Public relations officer. (1941, January 30). *The Argus*, p. 8.

Quarles, J., & Potts, D. (1990, September). Public relations education in Australia: A report prepared for the National Executive of the Public Relations Institute of Australia. Sydney, Australia: Public Relations Institute of Australia.

Rea, J. (2002, July). *The feminisation of public relations: What's in it for the girls?* Paper presented at the meeting of Australia and New Zealand Communication Association, Gold Coast, Queensland. Retrieved from http://www.anzca.net/conferences/conference-papers/41-adam.html

Rutzou, D. (2010, September 1). Enthusiasm for public relations [Blog post]. *PR Blog: Dennis Rutzou Public Relations*. Retrieved from http://www.drpr.com.au/public-relations-blog/2010/09/01/enthusiasm-for-public-relations/

Talkabout. (1954, June 22). *The Argus*, p. 6.

Tasmanian secretary. (1969, March/April). *Public Relations Australia*, p. 13.

That list. (1956, July). *Pro-Files*, pp. 6–7.

The speakers. (1966, March). Public relations in a shrinking world: March 10–13. *Public Relations Journal*, pp. 11–17.

The weekly Round. (1959, June 3). *The Australian Women's Weekly*, p. 2.

Third national public relations convention. (1969, March/April). Public relations: Performance and prospects [Convention theme]. *Public Relations Australia* [4-page supplement].

Traveller to display wardrobe. (1954, August 13). *The Newcastle Sun*, p. 12.

Vic. membership. (1970, February/March). *Public Relations Australia*, p. 6.

Welcome to eight new members. (1984, September). *Profile: The Newsletter of the Public Relations Institute of Australia (WA)*, p. 3.

What we're doing and saying. (1956, March/April). *P.R. News*, p. 6.

Witz, A. (1992). *Professions and patriarchy*. London, UK: Routledge.

Wool wings its way around the world. (1959, June 3). *The Australian Women's Weekly*, p. 11.

Yaxley, H. M. L. (2013). Career experiences of women in British public relations (1970–1989). *Public Relations Review, 39*(2), 156–165. doi:10.1016/j.pubrev.2013.03.009.

Zawawi, C. (2009). A history of public relations in Australia. In J. Johnston & C. Zawawi (Eds.), *Public relations: Theory and practice* (3rd ed., pp. 26–46). Crows Nest, Australia: Allen & Unwin.

CHAPTER 4

Globalization, History, and Australian Expertise

Abstract In this much-needed account of the impact of globalization on Australian public relations, Fitch reveals the significance of transnational and international activity from the mid-twentieth century. Despite an emphasis on US public relations in Australian public relations education and history, the early institutes sought to align with the UK institute. The Australian industry was always international in outlook in that global mobility, international trade, and colonial networks were prominent. Asia was a significant market for Australian public relations, but the "othering" of Asian public relations enabled the Australian industry to claim superiority. Conceptualizations of public relations knowledge and expertise were framed within the dominant paradigm, even as Australian public relations was perceived as "unique." This chapter offers new insights into the construction of a professional occupational identity along national lines.

Keywords Asia • Australia • Globalization • International • Occupational identity • Public relations

© The Editor(s) (if applicable) and The Author(s) 2016   87
K. Fitch, *Professionalizing Public Relations*,
DOI 10.1057/978-1-137-57309-4_4

INTRODUCTION

Chapter 1 argued that public relations histories tend to be shaped by particular ideologies that support a narrow conceptualization of public relations, and therefore are understood in terms of a linear progression towards professional status. It identified a need for more critical histories of public relations. This chapter develops these ideas in relation to the construction of both public relations as a profession and a professional occupational identity. Building on the significance of education and gender, explored in Chaps. 2 and 3, for the development of such an identity, this chapter investigates the impact of global and transnational activity. It reviews historical narratives of public relations in the twentieth century, which suggest US public relations activity was influential in the development of Australian public relations. It also explores the links between Australian and British public relations institutes. This chapter then investigates Australian public relations activity in the Asian region and how such activity informed the construction of a professional occupational identity for Australian public relations. Finally, it considers the significance of transnational and international activity for understanding the historical development of Australian public relations.

GLOBALIZATION AND AUSTRALIAN PUBLIC RELATIONS HISTORY

Historical Narratives and International Engagement

Much public relations history explores the development of public relations along national lines—the recent National Perspectives series (Watson, 2014–2015) is a typical example. The chapters are primarily organized around development within one or more countries and tend to ignore transnational, regional, and global activity. Despite an increasing emphasis on sociocultural perspectives on public relations in the last decade, few scholars have explored the impact of globalization, in terms of regional and transnational activity, on public relations history. Australian histories of advertising, marketing, and other promotional industries have begun to consider global activity (Dickenson, 2014), but there is yet to be similar investigations of public relations history, other than isolated acknowledgements, articles, and book chapters exploring the role of IPRA (Watson & Macnamara, 2013), the internationalization of education (Fitch, 2013), and

the activities of the Empire Marketing Board in promoting Australian produce (Sheehan, 2007; Anthony, 2012) or identifying Eric White Associates'
(EWA) expansion into Asia (Griffen-Foley, 2012; Sheehan, 2010). Instead,
as shown in Chap. 1, the historical development of Australian public relations is primarily conceptualized as emerging from US military information
activity during World War II and the post-war establishment of professional
institutes; these understandings ignore both earlier public relations activity
and Australian industry engagement with other countries.

It is difficult to know precisely how such significance was assigned to the
World War II arrival of General MacArthur and his public relations team
and why such a belief has persisted in contemporary accounts of Australian
public relations history. It may be partly due to the experiences of Asher
Joel, who received the Order of the British Empire for services to social
welfare and charitable organizations (Sparrow & Fawsitt, 1956, p. 7) and
was knighted in 1971; from 1958 to 1978, he was a member of the NSW
Legislative Council (Parliament of NSW, n.d.). He was a journalist and a
publicity officer prior to World War II, and in 1944–1945 was seconded to
General MacArthur's staff in the Philippines and later claimed that he "was
often the only Australian in the area," "even lost his Australian accent,"
and "represented Australia 'off his own bat'" (Thomson, 1956, p. 2).
The author of one *P.R. News* profile declared Joel a "fair dinkum Aussie"
(Thomson, p. 1). At the end of the war, Joel set up a consultancy, and
later claimed to be the first Australian elected to PRSA. The significance of
MacArthur's legacy for Australian public relations, then, appears to ema-
nate from Asher Joel. The idea that MacArthur brought public relations—
with its focus on "news management" as opposed to simply publicity—to
Australia is persistent, and is reproduced in textbooks and PRIA-endorsed
accounts. Zawawi, for instance, acknowledges the "strong influence" of US
public relations on Australian public relations, but much of her information
appears to be based on a personal interview with Joel in 1995 (2009, p. 26).
Similarly, Harrison claims "US pioneers of the new profession led the way"
and "General Douglas MacArthur introduced the term 'public relations'
to Australia" (2011, p. 51, 65). In recent years, Australian scholars have
shown that public relations activity was well established in Australia prior to
World War II (see Macnamara & Crawford, 2010; Sheehan, 2007, 2014).

Despite Australia's colonial history, geographical location in the Asian
region, and explicit government multicultural policies, the impact of a
mainstream Anglo, white culture on the development of public relations in
Australia has not been researched. This lack may stem from the dominant

paradigm for public relations, which emphasizes functionalist and managerialist perspectives and promotes public relations as a universal practice, thereby ignoring the sociocultural contexts, in particular for US studies, which contributed to that paradigm (L'Etang, 2008a; Munshi & Edwards, 2011). Indeed, the belief that public relations was an American invention was widespread even in the mid-twentieth century: an address given at a PRSA conference and reported in an Australian industry newsletter in the mid-1950s stated that "Public relations—which is about as American as Thanksgiving turkey—has now spread to the far corners of the free world, and it's going strong" (Leffingwell, 1956). Critical race and postcolonial scholars argue public relations is institutionally racist due to its historical roots in colonial structures and capitalism and its role in maintaining the power structures of political and business elites (Edwards, 2013; Munshi & Edwards, 2011). Consequently, there is limited empirical research into Australian public relations activity across borders in the Asian region, or into how such activity may have influenced the historical development of public relations in Australia.

This chapter argues that the Australian industry was outward looking from its early years albeit along imperial and colonial lines. Despite evidence of extensive Australian public relations activity in the Asian region, the early Australian professional institutes' focus was primarily public relations in the UK and the USA. Regional activity had only a limited impact on the development of an Australian professional occupational identity. Chap. 2 identified the significance of international students, primarily from countries in Asia, for the growth of public relations education in Australia from the 1980s onwards and some industry concerns that more information on Australia's Asian trading partners should be included in public relations curricula. It also established that US textbooks and accreditation guidelines for university courses were widely adopted in Australia in the 1980s and 1990s. Chap. 3 identified the significance of global mobility for careers in public relations throughout the second half of the twentieth century. This chapter, then, considers whether international influences, experiences, and engagement contributed to understandings of a uniquely Australian public relations occupational identity.

"We'll Soon Be British"

Although the USA is considered to provide the template for modern public relations, archival evidence confirms that the fledgling Australian institutes, and particularly PRIA (Vic), had strong ties with IPR in Britain, which was established in 1948. In fact, in its early years the Victorian institute appeared more focused on establishing links with IPR than with the NSW institute, AIPR (Amalgamation, 1953; NSW Approach Us, 1953). PRIA (Vic) even sought formal affiliation with the British institute, reporting in its first year that "as one of our members insisted at a recent dinner, we must strive to be British" (We'll Soon Be British, 1952, p. 2). IPR responded that its constitution did not allow for overseas affiliations; nevertheless, they put PRIA (Vic) on their mailing list and forwarded their constitution, membership list, quarterly journal and annual report (British Institute, 1953). In 1954, IPR invited Victorian institute members to send a representative to their conference and, more significantly, to apply for overseas membership (First Public Relations, 1954). By the mid-1950s, IPR was actively recruiting Australians as overseas members from Victoria, noting that the subscription was tax deductible and included their "excellent quarterly publication" (IPR London, 1956, p. 4).

British public relations activities were frequently reported in the Australian institute journals in the 1950s and 1960s, such as a report from *The Advertiser's Weekly* about the annual conference in 1953, which included IPR president Sir Stephen Tallents's presentation on technological developments in media and the importance of visual media (Grand Alliance, 1953); the formation of IPRA in Bath in 1955 (International P.R. Association, 1955); IPR's financial difficulties following the introduction of a membership examination (Hard Times for IPR, 1967); and the suspension of two members for ethical breaches (UK Suspensions, 1967). The Australian journals reproduced articles such as "The Film as Public Relations Medium" (Trusler, 1966) from the *British Public Relations Journal* and other British industry publications, and promoted books from the Institute of Public Affairs in London (For Your Bookshelf, 1966).

Emerald Goetze (1956), a PRIA (Vic) committee member who worked as a public relations officer at the Victorian School of the Deaf and later as appeals director at St John's Homes for Boys, reported on her participation in IPR's monthly luncheon in London, after she was formally elected an Overseas Associate member. Goetze expressed surprise at having to pay for her pre-luncheon sherry, which was not included in the luncheon cost. She estimated there were 120 people (of approximately 700 IPR members) present and that "a goodly proportion of them were women." While in London, she also visited television studios, the Aldwych Press Club, and the Central Office for Information. Goetze observed government public relations seemed more prominent in the UK than in Australia, although "comparatively, Melbourne has more P.R. personnel employed by private enterprise" and that in the UK there was "a certain prejudice against women in PR jobs, and yet the smaller women consultants seem to get even more business than the men" (1956, p. 18).

Industry news sections in *P.R. News* and *Pro-Files* detail members' extended visits to the UK and their intention to meet with representatives of the British public relations industry. For example, Noel Griffiths, foundation president of both AIPR and the national institute, planned to spend his six-month long service leave in Europe and visit IPR in London (What We're Doing, 1955). On his retirement, Griffiths claimed, presumably in relation to an earlier visit, he "even met members of the newly-formed English P.R Institute and arrived back in Australia armed with a copy of that body's constitution and a determination to get a similar organisation" (Profile: Noel Griffiths, 1965). Outside of professional institutes, there were opportunities to network with public relations colleagues in similar sectors; John Ulm, Chief Press and Information Officer for Qantas, for example, chaired a four-day public relations conference of the International Air Transport Association in Paris (Stanger, 1965a) and, similarly, L.M. Boone, public relations officer for the Department of Local Government planned to contact local government public relations officers in England during his seven-month trip (What We're Doing, 1955). Chap. 3 identified the significance of global mobility for women's careers in public relations both before and after World War II. A typical story in the social pages of a local paper reports a luncheon given by Kitty Giles, public relations officer for a large Western Australian department store, Boans Ltd, prior to her departure to travel to England and pictures both Gillies and her temporary replacement (Public Relations Luncheon, 1950). Not all travel to the UK was for leisure, as working in London was a well-trodden path for Australian practitioners. Throughout the 1960s and 1970s, institute journals reported postings to the London offices of multinational companies and members' employment in the public relations industry in London. Scholars of advertising history have observed the significance of overseas travel for Australian practitioners in these decades in that it signified both personal and professional achievement (Crawford & Dickenson, 2014).

US Versus Australian Expertise

The US public relations industry, through the expansion of consultancies and individual practitioners, did play a role in the development of the local industry. In addition to Asher and Joe Joel's experiences with the US military and US companies such as RKO Radio Pictures and Columbia Pictures, respectively, Hill & Knowlton established an Australian office in Sydney in 1954 and employed an American, George E. McCadden, who had already worked in Australia for seven years, to manage the Caltex account (Miller, 1999). The Sydney-based AIPR was interested in American public relations with more than one member maintaining PRSA membership. American practitioners worked in Australia, and, like Hill & Knowlton, American companies had Australian clients and established offices in Australia (Miller, 1999). Hill & Knowlton took over EWA in the mid-1970s, although EWA continued to trade under its own name into the 1980s (Watson & Macnamara, 2013).

In terms of education, as discussed in Chap. 2, the introduction of a formal, national accreditation programme was modelled on PRSA guidelines and the use of US textbooks in Australian courses was widespread. Further, it is worth noting that various members of PRIA's National Education Committee (NEC), established in 1991 and responsible for the accreditation of university courses, had strong US connections: Marjorie Anderson had worked as social secretary at the Australian High Commission in Washington for almost two decades; David Potts was a visiting scholar at American universities; and Jan Quarles was an American academic who taught at RMIT in the early 1990s. Australian courses such as certificate and associate diploma courses introduced at RMIT in 1964 and 1967, respectively, were modelled on a public relations course at Boston College's School of Communication (Gleeson, 2014). Visiting academics, mostly from the US, came to Australia either on lecture tours or as invited conference speakers as early as 1968 (Lerbinger in Australia, 1968). James Grunig (2007) maintains he made 52 presentations in Brisbane, Sydney, Bathurst, Canberra, Melbourne, Hobart, Adelaide, and Perth, including 12 university presentations and gave the Noel Griffiths Memorial Lecture at Parliament House in Sydney, as part of a month-long tour with PRIA's "Visiting Eminent Practitioner" programme in 1996.[1] Under the same programme, Larissa Grunig (2006) gave 30 presentations to consultancies, student groups, universities, and executive women's groups. Their presentations focused on the key findings of the International Association of Business Communicators [IABC]-funded excellence study (Special PRIA State, 1996).

However, in the 1980s and 1990s, there is growing evidence in PRIA archives of a desire for Australian public relations expertise to be recognized as unique. Chap. 2 identified requests for more Australian resources and case studies to inform the university curriculum and the need to incorporate practitioner perspectives through, for example, guest lectures and practitioner-in-residence programmes. The College of Fellows requested changes to PRIA's "Eminent Visiting Practitioners" programme, following the national tour of Larissa and James Grunig to Australia in 1996, which resulted in a financial loss for the PRIA National Board in the region of $7–10,000.[2] In addition, individual state councils lost money although the national council agreed the visit had been successful and generated considerable media coverage. The Fellows requested that in future, "the program should include local eminent practitioners," noting "overseas practitioners did not have to [be] brought in every year and the program could include 'outstanding Australian practitioners.'"[3] The visiting practitioners programme subsequently included a combination of local and overseas practitioners.[4] The following year, Potts and Peter Lazar, as high-profile Australian practitioners and Fellows, toured several states under the programme; Potts also conducted senior professional assessments for members seeking regrading as part of this tour (Visitors Add Value, 1997). The Fellows sought therefore to have their expertise as senior practitioners with a unique understanding of the Australian context to be better recognized. From their perspective, Australian public relations knowledge was unique and derived from industry practice in Australia, and the Fellows were therefore the experts in Australian public relations.

Australia and IPRA

IPRA was established in May 1955, following earlier meetings between Dutch and British practitioners (L'Etang, 2004; Watson, 2011). Australians were interested in IPRA in its early years, with reports in Australian institute newsletters of IPRA activities, London-based Australian practitioners participating in IPRA meetings in Europe from 1959, and as reported in Chap. 1, Australian practitioners such as Noel Griffiths served on the IPRA Council in the early 1960s (Watson & Macnamara, 2013). Melbourne consultant Jon Royce was IPRA president in 1985, and played a pivotal role in Melbourne hosting the 11th Public Relations World Congress in

1988 (Planning in Hand, 1985). Watson and Macnamara (2013) argue the congress represented a significant development for the Australian public relations industry in that Australian membership and leadership roles peaked in IPRA in the early 1990s. Sydney consultant and former PRIA president, Jim Pritchett, joined the IPRA board and became president in 1992. Under Pritchett's presidency, Australians made up IPRA's third largest membership group. NEC member and RMIT academic Jan Quarles (1993) served on IPRA's education advisory council in the early 1990s.

In addition to international professional networks, IPRA's gold papers were useful for both professional associations and industry practitioners. A copy of *Gold Paper No. 7: Public Relations Education: Recommendations and Standards* (IPRA, 1990) is included in the Anderson archives, and used to justify the introduction of accreditation for university courses. Australians played a prominent role in the development of IPRA's (1994) *Gold Paper No. 11: Public Relations Evaluation.* Gael Walker and Sheila O'Sullivan were both NEC members in the 1990s, and two of five Australians involved in the development of the paper on research and evaluation (Watson & Macnamara, 2013).

According to L'Etang (2004), IPRA was established as an Anglophone organization that promoted primarily American and European perspectives. This Euro- and North American-centrism is notable in comments by former IPRA General Secretary (1989–1992) and President (1996), Roger Hayes, that in the 1980s Australia was "not really a major player on the international PR scene" and attributed the declining Australian membership to the country's geographic isolation, noting "there was never really any strong engagement (between) Australia and the rest of the world. It's still seen as an outpost" (cited in Watson & Macnamara, 2013, p. 7, 14). Watson and Macnamara concluded that Australians' major involvement in IPRA, which peaked in one decade, 1983–1993, "demonstrated rising national confidence and a desire to take a more outward look on international relationships" (2013, p. 15). However, claims that the Australian public relations industry was not previously international failed to recognize early links with UK and US institutes, the considerable global mobility of practitioners, as well as regional activity across Asia and other transnational activity in the second half of the twentieth century. Marketing, media, and advertising sectors are recognized at this time as increasingly international, with Australian agencies operating in Asia or servicing Australian and international clients across Asia from an Australian base (Sinclair, 1991).

"ASIA" AND AUSTRALIAN PUBLIC RELATIONS

Australia in Asia

Despite its geographical location, strong economic ties, and extensive trade links with various Asian countries, Australia has an ambivalent relationship with Asia in that its cultural heritage is primarily European, and in its imagined identity, is a "European outpost on the edge of Asia" inhabited by "'white' people" (Knight & Heazle, 2011, p. 221, 238). From the early years of the Victorian institute, John Handfield, as reported in Chap. 2, identified the need for public relations practitioners to be able to speak "an Asian language" and have an awareness of Asian politics and culture. However, as reported in the previous section, the primary focus of the institutes in the 1950s was on consolidating ties with Britain, and to a lesser extent, with the industry in the USA. But at the same time, there is evidence of increasing professional engagement with countries in Asia. I acknowledge "Asia" is a constructed, homogenizing, and contested term that refers to a large and diverse region. But Asia is central to the construction of the Australian identity "as a specially endowed, skilful and well governed people" and "as part of the prosperous 'West'" (Walker & Sobocinska, 2012, p. 12). This influence tends to be ignored in the construction of Australian histories, where Asia is persistently characterized as an important market offering new opportunities for Australian industry (Walker & Sobocinska, 2012).

The Commonwealth was significant in the development of government public relations throughout the region, with an article by the manager of the public relations department of the Hawaiian Sugar Planters' Association arguing that Britain surpassed the USA in government public relations: "In Hong Kong and Malaya, and in all British possessions, one finds excellent Public Relations Departments of the local government" (Leffingwell, 1956, p. 10). Articles in both NSW and Victorian institute newsletters reported on public relations activity in Commonwealth countries in the Asian region; see, for example, "The Ceylon Tea Industry and PR" (Read, 1956) by the Commissioner of the Tea Bureau for Australia and New Zealand and "PR in the Jungle" (1955) on the challenges of working in Malaya, Borneo and Brunei. Information was also provided on the industry in other countries in Asia (such as Public Relations Growth in Japan, 1966). PRIA (Vic) member, George Stapleton, managed a public relations campaign to commemorate the opening of a bulk fuel installation

at Nadi Airport in Fiji for Vacuum Oil; events included an official opening for 420 guests and the Governor of Fiji, a cocktail party, a vice-regal
luncheon, and a Fijian *tambua* ceremony for Vacuum Oil's managing
director (a ceremony traditionally reserved for kings and people of high
rank) (PR Job in Fiji, 1955).[5] The campaign attracted press coverage in
Fiji, Australia, and 20 other Pacific island centres and Stapleton produced
a souvenir publication. One guest speaker at a PRIA (Vic) luncheon
was Elizabeth Palmer, from the Young Women's Christian Association;
"between 1948 and 1951 she worked in Pakistan, India, Ceylon, Burma,
Malaya and Siam ... her experiences in South East Asia provide Miss
Palmer with authoritative material for her speech on the need for better
international relations with the Asian countries" (International Relations,
1954).

Public servants from countries within the Commonwealth visited
Australia, and were hosted by various public relations departments under
the Colombo Plan for Cooperative Economic Development in South and
Southeast Asia, which was established in 1950 and of which Australia was
a founding member. The plan enabled developed countries to promote
skill development and build capacity in developing countries. One AIPR
newsletter article discussed the challenges of doing public relations in
Colombo Plan countries, noting that "public relations really has to cope
with the primitive," given the "lack of press, radio, films, printing services,
public opinion survey and all the rest" along with the challenges of illit-
eracy (PR In The Jungle, 1955 p. 5):

> Your "public" lives in small isolated communal villages with few contacts
> with each. They have no papers, no radio and have never seen a film. Roads
> are non-existent and the only means of travel is on foot along jungle paths.
> Each village has its own dialect.
> ...
> All in all, the lot of the P.R. man in Malaya or any of its near East Indies
> neighbours isn't a particularly enticing one.

The same article reported that 30 East Indies public servants visited
Australia in 1955 under the Colombo Plan and participated in a public relations workshop run by AIPR vice president, Don Barnes. The
Colombo Plan proved pivotal in exchanging public relations knowledge
between Australia and various Asian countries over subsequent decades
as it evolved and expanded to include many more countries. The High

Commissioner for Malaysia, His Excellency Tun Lim Yew Hock, was a guest speaker at an institute luncheon in the 1960s and, in addition to paying "tribute to the help Australia was giving Malaysia in many forms and particularly in the higher education of more than 6000 Malaysian students now in Australia, many under the Colombo Plan," stated "we need more of your technical knowledge and management skill to help us diversify our economy" (High Commission, 1965; NSW Formal Luncheon, 1965). International practitioners were hosted by institute members in Australia and visited government departments and corporate public relations offices. For example, Indonesian Dr Goto Hendarto (who was somewhat insensitively renamed "Hank" by his Australian hosts) came to Australia for the second national public relations convention and then visited the Postmaster General to witness public relations training, learn about public relations films, and view the organization's theatrette (Colombo Plan Fellow, 1966). National conferences in the 1960s illustrate that the Australian industry sector was outward looking although primarily aligned with the West; for example, early promotion for the 1966 convention pointed to panels on "World Communications—Today and Tomorrow" and "Public Relations—International," which in advance promotion, pointed to unnamed speakers from the USA and UK (1966 National Convention Programme, 1965). The conference theme was "Public Relations in a Shrinking World" (1966), concerned with technological developments and their impact on communication.

Australian Practitioners in Asia

Australian practitioners and agencies were influential in the development of public relations in various cities in Southeast Asia, and possibly earlier than the 1960s' expansion of EWA identified by some scholars (see Sheehan, 2010), given evidence of Australian regional activity in the 1950s. But the international expansion of Australian consultancies, notably EWA, played a prominent regional role from the 1960s. From 1964 until 1974, when it was acquired by Hill & Knowlton, Australian public relations consultancy EWA focused increasingly on Asia, establishing a presence in Bangkok, Hong Kong, Jakarta, Kuala Lumpur, and Singapore to work with multinational oil companies and on government nation-building campaigns (Griffen-Foley, 2012). There is some evidence that the Bangkok office operated as a cover for the Australian Secret Intelligence Service from 1968 to 1975 (Griffen-Foley, 2012;

Sheehan, 2010). L'Etang (2004) identified that post-war decolonization contributed to significant growth in public relations activity internationally, and that individual practitioners found work with foreign governments (including "intelligence" operations) and with multinational companies keen to protect their overseas interests. EWA (1966) had offices in London, Birmingham, Wellington, Auckland, Hong Kong, Singapore, Kuala Lumpur, and seven Australian cities. Institute newsletters in the 1960s and 1970s frequently reported on members' postings to EWA overseas offices. In a 1968 book, *Handbook on International Public Relations*, EWA directors wrote chapters on public relations in Australia, Hong Kong, India, Indonesia, Japan, Malaysia, New Zealand, and Singapore (Hill & Knowlton International, 1968). EWA was a dominant force in the Australian public relations industry, and many industry "pioneers" and PRIA Fellows worked for EWA or International Public Relations, which was established by Laurie Kerr after he left EWA in 1964 (Morath, 2008; Most Powerful Man, 2002; Turnbull, 2010). The expansion into Asia was not restricted to EWA; Image Australia (1966) also promoted itself as having "associates in Manila and Auckland" and many Australian practitioners worked for multinational corporations and governments throughout the Asian region. For example, Asher Joel's brother Joe worked in an Australian public relations role as Publicity Director for RKO Radio Pictures and Columbia Pictures and executive vice president of Screen Gems, where he was responsible for the distribution of television programmes in Asia and Australia (Joe Joel, 1986; Sparrow, 1956). He was invited by the newly independent Papua New Guinea to establish a government public relations office in the 1970s (Joe Joel, 1986).[6]

Although the impact of multinational corporations and expatriate practitioners on the historical development of public relations in various Asian countries is well recognized (Chay-Németh, 2009; Sriramesh, 2004), it is less recognized how these individual practitioner experiences may have influenced the public relations industry in Australia. The opportunity to work in Southeast Asia enhanced the careers of individual practitioners, allowing them to gain valuable international and management experience. Interview participants in this study lived and worked in England, Hong Kong, Indonesia, Malaysia, New Zealand, Singapore, and the USA. Two participants, Bill Mackey and Kevin Smith, played prominent roles in state and national PRIA councils after working in Asia. Mackey worked in Singapore and Malaysia in the 1970s where he gained significant management experience. He described managing EWA in Singapore for three years:

> I had no idea, look at 29 you've got no idea about anything and I went to run an office with 10 or 12 people in it and I'd never run anything or managed anybody ... thank god we had some good local Chinese staff who actually did know what they were doing.

Although Mackey returned to Australia in 1980, he indicated government controls in countries such as Singapore, Indonesia, and Malaysia meant community protests and strikes were unlikely and acknowledged Australian practitioners working overseas "had this sort of arrogant view that South East Asia was not as highly developed as we were in these new issues." After working for a state premier who was instrumental in developing Asian markets for Australian resources, Smith returned to consulting in the 1970s. Hill & Knowlton appointed Smith as senior public relations advisor to the Indonesian government's National Development Information Office, where he worked for three years before returning to Australia in 1981 (PRIA, 2007). Smith noted that his experiences contributed to an international orientation in his work and, later, teaching; he stated Australia's "future is Asia."

Another practitioner, Ken Hickson, wrote an opinion piece in an academic journal, in which he explored ethical issues in Asia. Despite the introduction of Hickson as "an Australia-based strategic communications consultant with 40 years' experience in media and public relations in Asia Pacific, including 17 years in Singapore" (2004, p. 345), there is no other mention of Australia. Hickson primarily compared Asian practices with those in the UK and USA; further, Hickson argues practitioners' involvement in "setting higher standards of business practice, having open and transparent tender systems, and getting rid of 'crony capitalism' have all gone a long way to reduce rampant corruption in most Asian countries" (2004, p. 6). Underpinning this article is an assumption that Western practices are superior and more democratic than those practised in diverse Asian countries. This conceptualization of public relations is closely linked to a US-derived dominant paradigm and thereby poses challenges for public relations in Asia, which can never gain professional recognition or social legitimacy if it is measured against standards derived from Western, liberal-democratic, market economies (Fitch & Surma, 2006).

Expansion and Protectionism

In the 1980s and 1990s, more Australian-based public relations consultancies expanded into various Asian cities. Like the Australian advertising industry, which Crawford (2008) characterized the 1980s as the decade in which it became global, the 1980s saw much expansion and growing international activity. There are references in industry newsletters, for example, to a joint venture in the provision of public relations services, including press relations and monitoring, political briefings, and conference organization in China (Burson-Marsteller/Xinhua in China, 1985); the establishment and management of Hong Kong offices from Australia (Rush Sets Up in Hong Kong, 1989; H&K Asia to be managed from Australia, 1990); the expansion of Australia-based agencies into India and Sri Lanka (Expansion in India, 1993); and a delegation of senior PRIA members visiting China (Mission to China, 1996; Rebeiro, 1997). An unsuccessful proposal to host the IPRA conference in conjunction with PRIA National Convention in 1994 is explicit about the significance of the Asian region for the industry, in the face of perceived twin threats of the unified single market in Europe (described as "Fortress Europe") and the growth in production in the East Asian region, "with the emergence of Newly Industrialised Economies such as Hong Kong, Singapore, Korea, Taiwan, China, Indonesia, Malaysia and Thailand as well as the dynamic economy of Japan."[7] Asia was recognized in these industry newsletters and in the proposal as a significant region for international trade, particularly in terms of declining market opportunities in Europe.

While Asia was constructed as a significant market for Australian public relations activity, in line with the persistent trope identified by Walker and Sobocinska (2012), one PRIA member was keen to restrict Asian practitioners working in Australia. In what can only be construed as protectionism for Australian practitioners, the writer cited Australian Bureau of Statistics figures in a PRIA newsletter to criticize the Australian government's Independent Migrant programme:

A quick breakdown of the various countries from which the 178 public relations officers came in 1995 show that 61 came from Hong Kong, 27 came from India, 24 came from the UK and Ireland, 19 came from China and the balance from countries such as Sri Lanka, Malaysia and Singapore. To put it mildly, public relations officials from India, the People's Republic of China or Hong Kong are not in a good position to compete in a marketplace where local knowledge and networks, plus good English are crucial. (Morton-Evans 1996, p. 9)

Public relations expertise is conceptualized as dependent on local professional contacts and experience, suggesting that only expertise derived in the Australian industry adequately prepares practitioners for Australian practice. In another example, an applicant with significant overseas experience at senior levels was rejected for full PRIA membership in 1997. Following consultation with PRIA's national examiner, the chair of PRIA's State Admission Board informed the candidate "that you require some experience in the Australian context before regrading."[8] Although the candidate's experience was not specifically in Asia, this correspondence suggests that from the perspective of the professional association, the Australian context is unique and therefore Australian experience, personal contacts or networks, and local knowledge are more important than experience gained elsewhere. However, these decisions were not consistent; over a decade earlier, when state councils were responsible for the admission of members, a former vice president of Singapore's IPRS was offered professional-grade membership when he migrated to Western Australia in 1984 (Welcome to Eight, 1984). This shift in membership processes illustrates the impact of stricter requirements for professional-grade members from 1985. Although the written criteria did not demand Australian industry experience, there were, in practice, clear expectations around the need for Australian social and cultural capital, in the sense of personal networks and local knowledge, in order to be admitted to professional membership ranks. Further, applicants had to be proposed and seconded by existing professional-grade members, confirming the significance of existing Australian industry networks for admission into PRIA's exclusive membership ranks.

Australian Education: Markets and Influences

As discussed in Chap. 2, many countries in Asia became important markets for Australian universities and contributed to the significant growth in Australian public relations courses from the late 1980s. Changes in government education policy in 1987 and 1994 allowed international fee-paying students to come to Australia, and Australian universities increasingly offered their courses internationally (Fitch, 2013). The growth in international student numbers, partly in response to the need for universities to find new revenue sources, led to active engagement with education institutions in countries such as India, Indonesia, Hong Kong, Malaysia, Singapore, and Vietnam. Australian educators also made links with public relations associations in those countries. An educator wrote to PRIA's NEC that the Australian industry, as "a regional leader" had a responsibility "to help develop the profession and the professional competencies of practitioners" in Asia.[9]

There is little evidence that either the changing student cohort or transnational public relations activity had a significant impact on PRIA expectations of university education, following the introduction of a standardized, national course accreditation programme in 1991. A focus on Asia was not part of the formal, written PRIA course accreditation criteria, which were adapted from PRSA guidelines, but was occasionally requested by education panels assessing university courses. This feedback varied between states and was inconsistent as to whether an Asian or more global focus was needed. Often, comments related to significant trading partners for Australia, which in the 1990s was Japan. However, PRIA education committees expressed concern over a lack of English competency among international students and requested universities provide additional language support. Both these examples reflect concerns that education should train students to meet the demands of Australian employers. Despite evidence of significant transnational and regional public relations activity, knowledge and competencies required to operate in the Asian region, or, indeed, in the broader global context, were not addressed in PRIA course accreditation, which focused primarily on a national curriculum. It is worth noting the Australian textbook *Practising public relations: A case study approach* (Quarles & Rowling, 1993) did highlight the need for intercultural competence among Australian practitioners and drew on Asian case studies.

The focus on public relations education meeting the needs of the national professional association points to the underlying assumption of Australian public relations as unique even as practitioners worked in an increasingly global environment. While the widespread use of US textbooks was acknowledged as useful for theory, they were considered less useful in developing students to be Australian practitioners. Attempts to define Australian public relations as advanced in comparison to the rest of the world suggest senior PRIA members sought to establish Australian public relations practice as unique and themselves, as the experts and the repository of Australian public relations knowledge. However, US studies and resources framed and dominated the conceptualization of Australian public relations, even though the analysis of the Anderson archives and participant interviews points to a widespread recognition of their limitations for the Australian context.

DEVELOPING A PROFESSIONAL OCCUPATIONAL IDENTITY

Professionalization, Ethnicity, and Race

Professional associations play a major role in the construction of a normative occupational identity, particularly in service industries such as public relations that struggle to gain social legitimacy and professional recognition (Edwards, 2014a). Disciplinary discourses construct practice and occupational identity and thereby contribute to exclusionary processes of occupational closure (Edwards, 2014a, 2014b). The majority of professional association activities seek to establish jurisdiction over public relations activity through, for instance, the regulation of education and training, and entry into its senior membership ranks. There is also a less formal credentialling that occurs in relation to both pathways into public relations and advancement in careers. Recognizing that a strategic occupational identity is socially constructed (Ashcraft, Muhr, Rennstam, & Sullivan, 2012), the construction of this professional identity assumes particular characteristics or traits. Writing on gender, Davies argues professionalism demands "a conceptual framework that requires, but denies it requires, the Other" (1996, p. 672). Extending Davies's work, Ashcraft, Muhr, Rennstam, and Sullivan theorize that "without encoding gender and race hierarchy into its very profile, an occupation tends not to become or remain a profession" (2012, p. 471). Critical race scholars argue, for example, that "racialization in PR, then, begins with how the occupation constructs its jurisdiction and argues its legitimacy" (Edwards, 2014b, p. 48) and race is "firmly embedded in the context and practice of PR" (Munshi & Edwards, 2011, p. 349).

Racial hierarchies are evident in language used in early institute journals, such as the brief report that Graham Kingsford-Smith was shipwrecked off Papua, and was one of "two European survivors and six natives" (Former PR Man, 1955). Of interest is how questions of occupational fit were underpinned by particular assumptions around "suitability" to enter the industry (such as the "good manners" and cultural knowledge identified by John Handfield in the early 1950s in Chap. 1) and related to the construction of public relations national knowledge and expertise along racial and ethnic lines. The dominance of an Anglo heritage and questions of occupational fit for the developing public relations industry in Australia are illustrated in a brief 1965 industry news story, which reported the appointment of South Australian institute council member, Fred Witsenhuysen, as the public relations officer at the Department of Supply (Stanger, 1965b). The author noted that Witsenhuysen "was chosen from 95 applicants and is believed to be the first non-British migrant to get a Commonwealth PRO job" (Stanger, 1965b, p. 4); in fact, Witsenhuysen, an Australian university graduate, was hardly a new migrant having arrived in Australia in 1951, gained citizenship in 1956, and worked as a journalist in Holland, Indonesia, and Australia before transitioning into public relations work.

The changing demographics of Australian society are relevant in terms of contextualizing such assumptions around occupational fit. Migration trends in Australia in the second half of the twentieth century demonstrate significant ties with the UK and Ireland, although migration from those countries steadily decreased from 73% in 1947 to 42% in 1961 and 31% in 1991; migrants from southern Europe dominated in the 1960s (Australian Bureau of Statistics[ABS], 1994). Explicit government policies on multiculturalism and the end of the "white Australia policy" in relation to immigration policies were introduced by the Whitlam government in the early 1970s and by the late 1980s, four of the top six countries for migration to Australia were in Asia (ABS, 1994). Since then there has been widespread recognition of cultural diversity within Australia, particularly around the significance for communicating to publics.

A special issue of PRIA's short-lived national journal, *The PRofessional*, on community relations offers some insights into a West/non-West binary in relation to public relations activity in the final decade of the twentieth century (Berryman, c. 1996). The cover features illustrations of racialized "otherness," that is, of non-white people, firmly equating concepts of community with diversity and confirming Munshi and Edwards's findings that race is implicit in public relations theory and practice, and implicit in business where "racialized others were deemed to be of value" (2011, p. 352). The first article discusses the development of communication campaigns with culturally diverse groups in Australia's multicultural society, stating that "public relations is able to transcend linguistic and cultural barriers" (Assaf, c. 1996, p. 8). It is followed by "Marketing Financial Services To The Multicultural Market" (Alexander, c. 1996). In another article, the

President of Asia Pacific for Edelman Public Relations Worldwide identified significant opportunities for Australian public relations practitioners in Asian markets and suggested Sydney become "a regional hub for public relations programs" (Sefiani, c. 1996, p. 14). The president cited "the Australian advantage" as "public relations is a highly developed craft in Australia with all the skills and services available in Europe or North America" and that Australian practitioners have "great experience in the kinds of programs that are needed by government and business in Asia." From the Australian industry perspective, then, public relations in Asia remained inferior to public relations in Western countries.

Australian Knowledge and Expertise

The research reported in this chapter reveals far more about the Australian industry than it does about Asia and offers some evidence of the impact of a dominant Western paradigm on conceptualizations of public relations and of Australia's white, Anglo cultural heritage in determining occupational fit. This chapter argues that renewed PRIA concerns in the 1980s and 1990s to unify various state-based councils and to establish professional standing contributed to the conceptualization of Australian public relations as not only unique but superior to practices in Asia. The predominantly Anglo heritage of Australia and the widespread influence of a dominant paradigm drawn from US studies significantly influenced this conceptualization. Further, international engagement through participation in IPRA only confirmed the desire to align Australian public relations expertise with American and European practices. At the same time, the industry sought to negotiate its professional identity in relation to Australia's dominant Anglo heritage, government multicultural policies, and the re-orientation of Australia towards countries in Asia that were both geographic neighbours and significant trading partners. There was no reference to Australian Indigenous culture or Indigenous public relations activity in the institute journals in the twentieth century.

In seeking a professional identity, the professional association sought to establish the Australian industry as unique, aligned to international standards of practice in the UK and the USA, and superior to public relations in Asia. However, this conceptualization was founded on an understanding of public relations drawn from the dominant paradigm and as a Western business practice. Despite evidence of extensive public relations activity in Asia through individual Australian practitioners, multinational corporations, and public relations consultancies, Australia–Asia trade, and the export of Australian public relations education, there is little evidence alternative conceptualizations of public relations were informed by this regional or transnational activity. Asia–Australia interactions are marginal in historical accounts of the development of Australian public relations. Rather, from the establishment of Australian public relations institutes, the Australian industry was constructed as superior to industries in Asia and, as part of its bid for professional recognition, sought an alliance primarily with British and the US public relations industries.

Comparison with practices in Asia only served to establish the uniqueness and "advanced" state of Australian public relations. Although individual practitioners recognized the value of their experience in Asia for their careers, particularly in terms of developing management expertise, this experience did not significantly inform the construction of a professional occupational identity for Australian public relations. This finding has implications for the constitution of public relations knowledge in Australia. It suggests that the drive to establish a clear occupational identity, as part of PRIA's claim for social legitimacy, and, in turn, professional recognition, meant that an exclusionary identity was constructed. This identity was conceptualized as expertise gained in an Australian context, that is, as an Australian cultural capital founded on local networks and contacts. Only professional experience in the Australian industry was considered to adequately prepare practitioners for PRIA's professional-grade membership. The "othering" of Asia allowed Australian public relations to be conceptualized as superior and deserving of professional recognition. Personal experiences and trade within Asia failed to inform the conceptualization of an Australian public relations identity, even as increasing trade with countries in Asia—and fewer trade opportunities with the former British Empire—ensured the commercial success of public relations.

This chapter provided evidence that state institutes drew on international links to develop various mechanisms of professionalization, including cognitive mechanisms such as schooling, education, training, knowledge, skills, conferences, books, journals, and magazines. In the 1950s, PRIA (Vic) was particularly keen to associate itself with the British IPR, by reproducing their newsletter articles and promoting their journals, books, and conferences in Australia. AIPR took an interest in both the US and UK public relations industries, pointing to the success of public relations education at university-level, and listing, for example, the degree courses available in the USA. Individual state institute members also joined IPR and PRSA. Each state institute developed in its own way, although there were similarities and shared resourcing in later years of journals and conferences. There was not a uniform public relations industry across Australia, even after PRIA was officially established as a single, national organization in 1994. Gleeson (2014) noted that the Sydney-based AIPR's activities dominate Australian public relations history at the expense of developments in other states. Similarly, although writing on advertising history, Crawford (2015) identifies major differences between Sydney and Melbourne and argues that it is incorrect to assume that the Australian industry is monolithic.

Senior Australian practitioners, in particular, PRIA's College of Fellows, established in 1987, wanted greater recognition from universities regarding their unique expertise in public relations in Australia. Not only is public relations expertise defined by the Fellows' perceptions and experiences of public relations, but in the Australian context, this localized professional knowledge is deemed by senior PRIA members to be at least as, if not more, valuable than that of international academics. These findings confirm considerable resistance towards both scholarly learning and non-Australian industry experience among some senior practitioners. It also points to a conceptualization of public relations knowledge that is uniquely Australian and embedded in Australian industry practice. Australian public relations activity in Asia appeared to have limited, if any, impact on the construction of a regional, that is, Asian identity for Australian public relations despite the 1994 IPRA proposal and other claims to the strategic location of Australia within the region in the final decade of the twentieth century. During the period 1985–1999, PRIA, as part of its professionalization agenda, sought to establish itself as a national organization. In part, this strategy was to address PRIA's disparate state-based structure, where state councils tended to operate independently of the national council. The focus on regulating public relations activity nationally, particularly in light of state–national tensions, meant that the broader regional context in which the Australian industry operated was not addressed. As professionalization became more urgent, evident in the introduction of greater regulatory structures from the mid-1980s, the professional occupational identity of public relations became more exclusive.

The evidence presented in this chapter confirms that an Australian cultural capital underpinned the conceptualization of a professional identity for Australian public relations practitioners. Professional knowledge and expertise were founded on personal networks and local knowledge. The emphasis on national identity and practices, aligned with the "superior" practices of Western public relations, ignored the significant transcultural and transnational public relations activity throughout the Asian region. Experiences and trade within Asia failed to significantly inform the conceptualization of an Australian public relations identity, even as increasing trade with countries in Asia—and fewer trade opportunities with the former British Empire—ensured the commercial success of public relations. This chapter reveals ideologies underpinning professional understandings of public relations in Australia along national lines and within a broader global context. Significantly, the dominant paradigm, derived primarily from studies of US industry practice, continued to structure conceptualizations of Australian public relations knowledge and expertise. Further research into the assumptions encoded into this professional identity, exploring, for instance, race, gender, and ethnicity, is needed.

Although Watson and Macnamara concluded that Australians' major involvement in IPRA, which peaked in one decade, 1983–1993, was evidence of "a more outward look" (2013, p. 15), this chapter argues that the Australian public relations industry was always international in outlook. However, much of this transnational and international activity was concerned with colonial networks, Australian trade, and the global mobility of individual practitioners and did little to contribute to the development of a national occupational identity. Instead, through the efforts of the professional association, as identified in Chap. 1, the industry sought to align Australian public relations expertise with "the best in the world" (MacIntosh, 1986, p. 45). It is clear, then, that the professionalization drive sought alignment with Western-centric notions of public relations, primarily British and US industries, despite the considerable professional activity and the geographic location of Australia in the Asian region. Even as Asia was increasingly recognized as an important market for Australia, and therefore offered opportunities for Australian public relations activity and education, despite early assertions of the importance for the industry of Asian cultural awareness, the reality of professional activity in Asian countries throughout the second half of the twentieth century, and individual practitioners' employment in Asian countries, this transnational activity had limited impact on the development of a professional occupational identity along national lines.

NOTES

1. The lecture was published by PRIA: Grunig, J. E. (1996, August 1). *Public relations as a management function. The Noel Griffiths Lecture* [20 pp. booklet]. Sydney, Australia: Public Relations Institute of Australia (NSW).
2. PRIA Board. (1996, September 18). "2(xi). Council of the College of Fellows" and "9. Eminent visiting practitioners." *Minutes of the meeting of the PRIA Board*, p. 3, 4. PRIA (National) archives (Box 29, ML72/2144, Board 93, 94, 95, 97). Mitchell Library, Sydney, Australia.
3. PRIA Board. (1996, October 29). "12. Visiting eminent practitioners." *Minutes of the meeting of the PRIA Board held by teleconference*, pp. 2–3. PRIA (National) archives (Box 29, ML72/2144, Board 93, 94, 95, 97). Mitchell Library, Sydney, Australia.
4. PRIA Board. (1997, March 18). "9(i). Visiting Eminent Practitioner Program." *Minutes of the meeting of the PRIA Board*, p. 4. PRIA (National) archives (Box 29, ML72/2144, Board 93, 94, 95, 97). Mitchell Library, Sydney, Australia.
5. The *tambua* is the tooth of a sperm whale and in Fiji is presented as a symbolic welcome for distinguished guests as part of a *kava* ceremony (Stanley, 1985).
6. Papua New Guinea gained independence from Australia in 1975.
7. A proposed theme for 1994 IPRA conference Perth, Western Australia, November, 1994. (c.1992). PRIA (WA) archives. Perth, Australia.
8. Birks, A. (1997, December 5). "Membership regrading" [Letter to practitioner, reply to November 19 letter querying the lack of professional-grade membership]. S.A.B. General Correspondence 97/98. PRIA (WA) archives, Perth, Australia.
9. University. (1998, March 4). [Letter to Marjorie Anderson]. Anderson archives (File 2).

REFERENCES

1966 national convention programme. (1965, November/December). *Public Relations Journal*, p. 3.

Alexander, D. (c. 1996). Marketing financial services to the multicultural market. *The PRofessional: Issues on Communication, Corporate Affairs and Public Relations*, *1*(3), 11.

Amalgamation. (1953, July). *Pro-Files*, pp. 3–10.

Anthony, S. (2012). *Public relations and the making of modern Britain: Stephen Tallents and the birth of a progressive media profession*. Manchester, UK: Manchester University Press.

Ashcraft, K. L., Muhr, S. L., Rennstam, J., & Sullivan, K. (2012). Professionalization as a branding activity: Occupational identity and the dialectic of inclusivity-exclusivity. *Gender, Work & Organization, 19*, 467–488. doi:10.1111/j.1468-0432.2012.00600.x.

Assaf, J. (c. 1996). Communicating with diversity requires a diversity of communication. Public relations is the answer. *The PRofessional: Issues on Communication, Corporate Affairs and Public Relations, 1*(3), 8–10.

Australian Bureau of Statistics [ABS]. (1994, last updated May 9, 2006). *4102.0— Australian Social Trends, 1994.* Retrieved from http://www.abs.gov.au/AUSSTATS/abs@.nsf/2f762f95845417aeca25706c00834efa/e0a8b4f57a46da56ca2570ec007853c9!OpenDocument

Berryman, R. (1996). Editor's note. *The PRofessional: Issues on Communication, Corporate Affairs and Public Relations* [Special Issue: Marketing Communication], *1*(4), 4.

British institute. (1953, February). *Pro-Files*, p. 3.

Burson-Marsteller/Xinhua in China joint venture. (1985, October). *Profile: The Newsletter of the Public Relations Institute of Australia (WA)*, p. 4.

Chay-Németh, C. (2009). Becoming professionals: A portrait of public relations in Singapore. In K. Sriramesh & D. Verčič (Eds.), *The global public relations handbook* (2nd ed., pp. 155–174). Abingdon, England: Routledge.

Colombo plan fellow. (1966, May). *Public Relations Journal*, p. 3.

Crawford, R. (2008). *But wait, there's more ... A history of Australian advertising, 1900–2000.* Carlton, Australia: Melbourne University Press.

Crawford, R. (2015). A tale of two advertising cities: Sydney suits v. Melbourne creatives. *Journal of Australian Studies, 39*(2), 235–251. doi:10.1080/14443058.2015.1021706.

Crawford, R., & Dickenson, J. (2014). Advertising lives: Memoir and career. *History Australia, 11*(3), 134–156.

Davies, C. (1996). The sociology of professions and the profession of gender. *Sociology, 30*, 661–678. doi:10.1177/0038038596030004003.

Dickenson, J. (2014). Global advertising histories: An Australian perspective. *History Compass, 12*(4), 321–332. doi:10.1111/hic3.12151.

Edwards, L. (2013). Institutional racism in cultural production: The case of public relations. *Popular Communication: The International Journal of Media and Culture, 11*(3), 242–256. doi:10.1080/15405702.2013.810084.

Edwards, L. (2014a). Discourse, credentialism and occupational closure in the communications industries: The case of public relations in the UK. *European Journal of Communication, 29*, 319–334. doi:10.1177/0267323113519228.

Edwards, L. (2014b). *Power, diversity and public relations.* London, UK: Routledge.

Eric White Associates [EWA]. (1966, October/November). [Advertisement]. *Public Relations Journal*, p. 16.

Expansion in India. (1993, May). *Public Relations: The Official Journal of PRIA (NSW) and PRIA (VIC)*, p. 11.

Fitch, K. (2013). A disciplinary perspective: The internationalization of Australian public relations education. *Journal of Studies in International Education, 17*, 136–147. doi:10.1177/1028315312474898.

Fitch, K., & Surma, A. (2006). The challenges of international education: Developing a public relations unit for the Asian region. *Journal of University Learning and Teaching Practice, 2*(3), 104–113. Retrieved from http://ro.uow.edu.au/jutlp/vol3/iss2/4/

For your bookshelf. (1966, June). *Public Relations Journal*, p. 5.

Former PR man shipwrecked. (1955, April). *Pro-Files*, p. 9

Gleeson, D. J. (2014). Public relations education in Australia, 1950–1975. *Journal of Communication Management, 18*, 193–206. doi:10.1108/JCOM-11-2012-0091.

Goetze, E. A. (1956, June). PR in London. *Pro-Files, 3*(1), pp. 17–18.

Grand alliance for PR. (1953, September). *Pro-Files*, pp. 14–17.

Griffen-Foley, B. (2012). White, Eric (1915–1989). *Australian dictionary of biography*. Canberra, Australia: National Centre of Biography. Retrieved from http://adb.anu.edu.au/biography/white-eric-15809

Grunig, J. E. (2007, September). Vitae. Retrieved from http://comm.umd.edu/sites/comm.umd.edu/files/JGrunigCV.pdf

Grunig, L. S. (2006, September). Larissa Schneider Grunig [CV]. Retrieved from http://comm.umd.edu/sites/comm.umd.edu/files/LGrunigCV2.pdf

H&K Asia to be managed from Australia. (1990, November). *Public Relations: The Official Journal of PRIA (NSW) and PRIA (VIC)*, p. 15.

Hard times for IPR. (1967, March/April). *Public Relations Journal*, p. 7.

Harrison, K. (2011). *Strategic public relations: A practical guide to success*. South Yarra, Australia: Palgrave Macmillan.

Hickson, K. (2004). Ethical issues in practising public relations in Asia [Opinion]. *Journal of Communication Management, 8*(4), 345–353. doi:10.1108/13632540410807736.

High commission in a "selling speech." (1965, July/August). *Public Relations Journal*, p. 11.

Hill & Knowlton International. (1968). *Handbook on international public relations* (Vol. 2). New York, NY: Praeger.

Image Australia. (1966, October/November). [Advertisement]. *Public Relations Journal*, p. 16.

International P.R. association formed. (1955, August). *P.R. News*, p. 3.

International Public Relations Association [IPRA]. (1990, September). *Public relations education: Recommendations and standards* (Gold Paper No. 7). Report by the IPRA Education and Research Committee and the IPRA International Commission on Public Relations Education.

International Public Relations Association [IPRA]. (1994, November). *Public relations evaluation: Professional accountability* (Gold Paper No. 11). Geneva, Switzerland: Author.

International relations with Asia: Miss Elizabeth Palmer—Guest Speaker for November (1954, October/November). *Pro-Files, 2*(11), p. 2.

Joe Joel, Film Executive. (1986, January 28). [Obituary]. *Sydney Morning Herald*, p. 5.

Knight, N., & Heazle, M. (2011). *Understanding Australia's neighbours: An introduction to East and Southeast Asia* (2nd ed.). Port Melbourne, Australia: Cambridge University Press.

Leffingwell, R. (1956, January/February). Public relations around the world. *P.R. News*, pp. 8–10.

Lerbinger in Australia. (1968). *Public Relations Australia*, p. 7.

L'Etang, J. (2004). *Public relations in Britain: A history of professional practice in the 20th century*. Mahwah, NJ: Lawrence Erlbaum.

IPR London. (1956, June). *Pro-Files, 3*(1), p. 4.

MacIntosh, I. (1986, September 16). Professionalism heralds new era. *Australian Financial Review: Public Relations*, p. 45.

Macnamara, J., & Crawford, R. (2010). Reconceptualising public relations in Australia: A historical and social re-analysis. *Asia Pacific Public Relations Journal, 11*(2), 17–33.

Miller, K. (1999). *The voice of business: Hill & Knowlton and postwar public relations*. Chapel Hill, NC: University of North Carolina Press.

Mission to China. (1996, November). *Public Relations: The Newsletter of the Public Relations Institute of Australia (NSW, VIC, QLD)*, p. 1.

Morath, K. (2008). *Pride and prejudice: Conversations with Australia's public relations legends*. Elanora, Australia: Nuhouse Press.

Morton-Evans, M. (1996, October). Grave doubts about overseas PRs. *Public Relations: The Newsletter of the Public Relations Institute of Australia (NSW, VIC, QLD)*, p. 9.

Munshi, D., & Edwards, L. (2011). Understanding "race" in/and public relations: Where do we start and where should we go? *Journal of Public Relations Research, 23*(4), 349–367. doi:10.1080/1062726X.2011.605976.

NSW approach us on federal body. (c. 1953). *Pro-Files, 1*(3), pp. 1–5.

NSW formal luncheon. (1965, May/June). *Public Relations Journal*, p. 2.

Planning in hand for 1988 IPRA congress in Australia. (1985, May). *Profile: The Newsletter of the Public Relations Institute of Australia (WA)*, p. 1.

PR in the jungle. (1955, April). *P.R. News*, p. 5.

PR job in Fiji. (1955). *Pro-Files*, pp. 7–8.

Profile: Noel Griffiths. (1965, July/August). *Public Relations Journal*, pp. 6–7.

Public relations growth in Japan. (1966, January/February). *Public Relations Journal*, pp. 8–9.

Public relations in a shrinking world. (1966, March). [Conference program]. *Public Relations Journal*, pp. 18–19.

Public Relations Institute of Australia [PRIA]. (2007). Kevin Smith Testimonial Lunch. Retrieved from http://www.pria.com.au/sitebuilder/events/events/files/48816/priawakevinsmithtestimoniallunchregistration.pdf

Public relations luncheon. (1950, December 12). *The West Australian*, p. 20.

Quarles, J. (1993). Up from down under: Public relations education in Australia. *International Public Relations Review, 16*(4), 21–24.

Quarles, J., & Rowlings, B. (1993). *Practising public relations: A case study approach.* Melbourne, Australia: Longman Cheshire.

Read, K. A. H. (1956, May/June). The Ceylon tea industry & P.R. *P.R. News*, pp. 12–14.

Rebeiro, D. (1997, August). The role of PR in China. *Profile: The Newsletter of the Public Relations Institute of Australia (WA)*, p. 3.

Rush sets up in Hong Kong. (1989, October). *Profile: The Newsletter of the Public Relations Institute of Australia (WA)*, p. 4.

Sefiani, R. (c. 1996). Communicating in multicultural Asia. *The PRofessional: Issues on Communication, Corporate Affairs and Public Relations, 1*(3), 12–14.

Sheehan, M. (2007, November). *Australian public relations campaigns: A select historical perspective 1899–1950.* Paper presented at the meeting of Australian media traditions: Distance and diversity: Reaching new audiences. Bathurst, Australia. Retrieved from http://www.csu.edu.au/special/amt/publication/sheehan.pdf

Sheehan, M. (2010). Eric White. Retrieved from Public Relations Institute of Australia [PRIA] www.pria.com.au/aboutus/in–honour–2/eric–white

Sheehan, M. (2014). Australasia. In T. Watson (Ed.), *Asian perspectives on the development of public relations: Other voices.* Houndmills, England: Palgrave Macmillan.

Sinclair, J. (1991). The advertising industry in Australia: Globalisation and national culture. *Media Information Australia, 62*, 31–40.

Sparrow, M. (1956, January/February). What we're doing and saying. *P.R. News*, pp. 4–6.

Sparrow, M., & Fawsitt, J. (1956, May/June). What we're doing and saying. *P.R. News*, pp. 7–11.

Special PRIA state conference 1996 edition. (1996, September). *Profile*, pp. 1, 4.

Sriramesh, K. (Ed.). (2004). *Public relations in Asia: An anthology.* Singapore, Singapore: Thomson Learning.

Stanger, J. (1965a, March/April). People in public relations. *Public Relations Journal*, p. 10.

Stanger, J. (1965b, November/December). People in public relations. *Public Relations Journal*, pp. 4–5.

Stanley, D. (1985). *Finding Fiji.* Chico, CA: Moon Publications.

The first public relations convention ever held in Australia. (1954, April). *Pro-Files*, *2*(6), pp. 2–3.

The Most Powerful Man. (2002, January 21). *Crikey*. Retrieved from http://www.crikey.com.au/2002/01/21/the-most-powerful-pr-man-of-all/

Thomson, I. (1956, May/June). Meet the members: No. 2—Asher Alexander Joel OBE. *P.R. News*, pp. 3–6.

Trusler, C. (1966, January/February). The film as a public relations medium. *Public Relations Journal*, pp. 8–9.

Turnbull, N. (2010). *How PR works—But often doesn't*. Melbourne, Australia: N. S. & J. S. Turnbull. Retrieved from http://noelturnbull.com/wp-content/uploads/2010/06/How-PR-works-but-often-doesnt.pdf

UK suspensions. (1967, March/April). *Public Relations Journal*, p. 3.

Visitors add value to WA. (1997, November/December). *Profile*, p. 5.

Walker, D., & Sobocinska, A. (Eds.). (2012). *Australia's Asia: From yellow peril to Asian century*. Perth, Australia: UWA Publishing.

Watson, T. (2011). Archive of the International Public Relations Association. Bournemouth, England: The Media School, Bournemouth University. Retrieved from http://microsites.bournemouth.ac.uk/historyofpr/files/2011/11/IPRA-ARCHIVE.pdf

Watson, T. (Ed.). (2014–2015). National perspectives on the development of public relations: Other voices. Houndsmill, England: Palgrave Macmillan.

Watson, T., & Macnamara, J. (2013). The rise and fall of IPRA in Australia: 1959 to 2000. *Asia Pacific Public Relations Journal*. Retrieved from http://eprints.bournemouth.ac.uk/21225/

We'll soon be British. (1952, October). *Pro-Files*, pp. 1–2.

Welcome to eight new members. (1984, September). *Profile: The Newsletter of the Public Relations Institute of Australia (WA)*, p. 3.

What we're doing and saying. (1955, November–December). *P.R. News*, p. 20.

Zawawi, C. (2009). A history of public relations in Australia. In J. Johnston & C. Zawawi (Eds.), *Public relations: Theory and practice* (3rd ed., pp. 26–46). Crows Nest, Australia: Allen & Unwin.

Conclusion

This book has addressed a significant gap in the literature by exploring the processes of professionalization. Until now, the history of Australian public relations has been presented in terms of its development as a profession, that is, as an evolutionary progression towards professional status. As such, public relations tends to be conceptualized in normative and functionalist terms as an ethical practice and as a strategic management discipline underpinned by a body of knowledge. This book has shown that knowledge to be dynamic, contested, and socially constructed. The functionalist orientation of the dominant paradigm influenced Australian understandings of public relations as a profession and continues to influence discourses around public relations, despite the recent emergence in alternative paradigms and critical public relations scholarship. Using a critique of functionalism as a starting point, this book offers a revisionist account of public relations and professional practice in Australia.

The investigation of the historical development of public relations in the second half of the twentieth century in Australia examined societal factors that contributed to the construction of public relations as a modern profession. The focus on what is excluded and/or marginalized from professional understandings of public relations offers new insights into contemporary issues. This book therefore offers a more nuanced and dynamic account of the development of public relations that considers

© The Editor(s) (if applicable) and The Author(s) 2016   117
K. Fitch, *Professionalizing Public Relations*,
DOI 10.1057/978-1-137-57309-4

the broader social and global context and challenges conceptualizations of public relations as a profession. The exploration of questions relating to transnational activity, gender, and education reveals the construction of public relations knowledge and expertise along national and gendered lines, women's historical contributions to public relations (and its subsequent coding as feminine), and the significance of education for the professional project. Although this research offers a uniquely Australian perspective, the findings are nevertheless significant for both public relations history and historiography elsewhere.

KNOWLEDGE AND EDUCATION

The shifts in understanding public relations reveal that far from an evolutionary development towards the modern profession, public relations in Australia always suffered from a lack of definition and unclear boundaries with similar occupational practices concerned with promotional work. By definition, a profession must establish jurisdiction over a unique service or expertise and yet Dickenson (2016) acknowledges the interplay between advertising and public relations in her history of Australian advertising. The historical evidence offered in this book points to the difficulty in establishing a clear and coherent definition, the gap between "professional" definitions and the actual day-to-day work of public relations, and the messy and contested boundaries between public relations, advertising, and marketing. It may be useful to think of public relations more broadly as promotional work (A. Davis, 2013) or, in line with recent calls from scholars, public communication, as part of a broader conceptualization of public relations work that recognizes the interdependence between these fields but which also embraces other kinds of communication activity (Demetrious, 2013; L'Etang, 2016; Macnamara & Crawford, 2010b). The shifts in conceptualizing public relations, from initial attempts in the 1950s to distinguish it from publicity and advertising to later attempts to establish public relations as a strategic management function (and not journalism, publicity, marketing, or advertising), point to increasing professionalization.

Competing conceptualizations of public relations knowledge and expertise played out in education. While education and training are important mechanisms of professionalization, in that they define and legitimize the body of knowledge and offer the means to regulate membership (L'Etang, 1999; 2008a), the institutionalization of public relations in the academy was challenged by different factions within the professional association and from established and co-emergent disciplines. The findings reported in this book confirm the constitution of public relations knowledge and its institutionalization in the Australian academy were dynamic and contested and primarily offered universities, and in particular lower-status universities, the opportunity to develop new markets. The significant growth in communication studies in Australia in the late 1980s and 1990s confirms that the growth in public relations courses was not unique and did not offer evidence of professional recognition. From the industry perspective, expectations of education were informed both by practitioners' own experiences and their expectations as employers of future graduates. However, these understandings were also shaped by the dominant paradigm and the widespread use of US textbooks and theories, which promoted a professional discourse.

Through accreditation, PRIA defined a suitable curriculum in part by asserting what public relations was not; in their rejection of subjects such as journalism and media studies, the NEC sought to distance public relations from media relations and publicity. The shift to greater practitioner involvement in accreditation processes in the 1990s led PRIA to seek a stronger alliance with business, management, and even marketing, despite public relations' alignment primarily with communication studies in the Australian academy. Avoiding over-simplistic, binary oppositions between practice and theory and between industry and academy, this book acknowledges the positions of practitioner–educator–scholar are not fixed. But in interrogating existing knowledge structures, it reveals the conceptualization of public relations as a business and management practice in the final decades of the twentieth century was promoted by PRIA state councillors and the College of Fellows, who understood public relations education in terms of both providing a public relations workforce primarily for the corporate sector and, in tandem, its significance for the professional project.

The persistence of the trope relating to the "failure" of public relations education to meet industry needs relates to particular conceptualizations of knowledge and expertise. Industry leaders, for example, complain about university public relations education, using the same discourses this research has identified in relation to the 1970s, 1980s, and 1990s. Even specific word choices, such as "agencies are at the coal face" (Christensen, 2014), echo Potts and privilege understandings of public relations knowledge and expertise derived in practice.[1] Although the public relations curriculum could define the body of knowledge, considered necessary for professional recognition; however, this "knowledge" proved problematic for the professional association, in that its senior practitioners, particularly the Fellows, were the designated repository of Australian public relations expertise. This finding confirms UK and European studies, which found that for practitioners, public relations knowledge is experiential and constituted in practice (Pieczka, 2002; 2007) and focused on serving client and organizational interests (van Ruler, 2005). Given the disciplinary alliance of public relations primarily with communication in the Australian academy, then it may be that university-level public relations education may never meet the expectations of a professional association that frame the field as a business, management function. Outside of the professional association, the industry is transforming in response to widespread technological change, illustrating that far from fixed, the knowledge required to perform public relations is both dynamic and diverse. In a social media age, the skills employers seek are wide ranging and by no means unique to public relations.

WOMEN AND PUBLIC RELATIONS

This book has sought to recognize women's diverse contributions to the historical development of public relations in Australia. In doing so, it challenged existing histories and assumptions around male "pioneers" and "heroes" credited with establishing public relations as a "modern profession." To understand the significance of gender and professions, it is important to recognize the ways women have participated in public relations, particularly in relation to the growing demarcation between masculine/professional activity and feminine/technical or support activity (Davies, 1996). In addition, the global mobility of many female practitioners points to another crucial element in the professional project: class, and highlights the need for more critical research into the gendered construction of public relations beyond a simple male/female binary, more complex understandings of gender, and its intersections with, for instance, race, class, and sexuality, in the construction of occupational identities (Fitch, 2016a).

Women have participated in Australian public relations much longer than is generally recognized, with evidence of their employment in public relations and promotional work prior to World War II, and their active participation in professional institutes in their first decade.

Women's membership levels in professional institutes varied only slightly, hovering between 11% and 15%, from the early 1950s to the late 1960s. As Gower (2001) found, women initially had few barriers to participating in public relations work and individual women enjoyed successful careers in publicity, advertising, and promotional roles, across diverse sectors. But women were marginalized from many of the professionalizing mechanisms of the industry by the late 1960s. They were poorly represented in professional-grade and elite-level memberships, and they were hardly evident as expert speakers at institute conferences or chapter authors in institute-endorsed books. By 1970–1971, other than in Tasmania, state institutes had no women on their committees. Further, analysis of the representation of women in the pages of the institute journal produced between 1965 and 1972 revealed that women were rarely portrayed as expert practitioners but as wives, secretaries, and consumers. This marginalization of women from professionalizing fields is not unique to public relations. However, focusing on the exclusion of women from senior roles within the public relations industry potentially ignores the ways their inclusion allows a particular conceptualization of public relations as professional practice (Davies, 1996); for example, women's public relations work in these decades was often confined to gendered sectors, such as retail and women's interest accounts, as well as administrative support.

The rapid feminization of the Australian industry, which began in the 1970s, contributed to a gendered stratification between different kinds of public relations activity as professional and strategic versus non-professional and technical (Fitch & Third, 2014). The introduction of new membership categories, practitioner examinations, and accredited degrees from the mid-1980s aimed to ensure professional-grade membership and high-level public relations activity was demarcated from low-level activity and activity in non-corporate sectors. Anxiety about the growing feminization of the industry contributed to the introduction of new membership structures, greater regulation of the industry, and even helped structure conceptualizations of public relations knowledge and expertise along gendered lines (Fitch, 2016a; Fitch & Third, 2010, 2014). This gendering had significant implications for PRIA's expectations of university education in that it encouraged public relations to be conceptualized as a management function and strategic business discipline and not as the low-level promotional work often associated with more feminized spheres, such as fashion, hospitality, and marketing. By the end of the twentieth century, national surveys and articles in PRIA newsletters revealed ongoing concern about the industry's feminization, in terms of its potential impact on the field's professional status (see Mina, 1996; Fisk, 1998a; 1998b). The gendering of public relations remains a global issue, with professional associations in the twenty-first century alert to structural inequalities within the industry. Industry reports, for example, document the discrepancy in pay and status along gender lines, and articles in trade and news media express anxiety about the implications of the "pink ghetto" status of public relations (Fitch, 2016a).

GLOBALIZATION AND COLONIAL NETWORKS

Although the historical development of public relations in Australia is strongly linked with the US industry and the introduction of public relations during World War II, the evidence in this book offers an alternative perspective. Public relations activity in Australia was always international, albeit with a strong focus on Britain; even nineteenth and early twentieth century campaigns were transnational in that they promoted Australian produce in association with the Empire Marketing Board, immigration, and later tourism, to Australia (Anthony, 2012; Crawford & Macnamara, 2014; Sheehan, 2014a; 2014b). The significant links between Australia and Britain are minimized in discussions of the historical development of Australian public relations because of the primacy of the US narrative. This issue is not unique to Australia. L'Etang "reject[s] the notion that public relations was invented by the Americans and exported to the UK" in her account of public relations history in Britain (2004, p. 223). Yet, many of the national histories in Watson's (2014–2015) edited series fail to challenge that assumption. Given the Victorian institute sought affiliation with IPR in its early years, even prior to an alliance with the NSW institute, a different narrative emerges regarding the establishment of professional public relations institutes in Australia. Further, for decades, Australian practitioners worked in and travelled to Britain seeking to develop their careers and make links with practitioners and professional institutes in similar sectors. British practitioners also migrated to Australia.

The impact of this Anglo heritage in Australia needs to be addressed, particularly in relation to how the development of an exclusionary identity contributed to occupational closure and justified professional recognition

(Edwards, 2014a; 2014b). As Edwards noted in her book on power and diversity in public relations, assumptions around race, class, gender, and ethnicity in relation to occupational fit are often "unremarkable" (2014b, p. 49). It is significant, then, that the "first non-British migrant to get a Commonwealth PRO job" (Stanger, 1965b, p. 4) was considered news-worthy in an institute journal in 1965, given the practitioner was already working in public relations in Australia and a member of the public relations institute in South Australia. Migration trends in Australia in the second half of the twentieth century demonstrate significant cultural links with the UK and Ireland, yet increasing migration from countries in southern Europe in the 1950s and 1960s and in Asia from the 1970s show the changing cultural diversity of Australian society in the second half of the twentieth century (ABS, 1994; Knight & Heazle, 2011). The evidence presented in this book highlights the need for more research into whether these changes were reflected in the industry itself, given the particular kinds of social and cultural capital that historically inform career pathways. Diversity within public relations remains a global issue, and the ethnocentrism of public relations narratives is increasingly noted by postcolonial and critical race scholars. However, in contrast to the US and UK industries, there is little information specifically on diversity within the contemporary Australian public relations industry.

In seeking a professional occupational identity, professional associa-tions sought to establish the Australian industry as unique, aligned to the standards of practice in the UK and the USA, and superior to public relations in Asia in the second half of the twentieth century. However, this conceptualization was founded on an understanding of public rela-tions drawn from the dominant paradigm and as a Western business practice. Further, as knowledge was conceptualized as emerging from Australian industry practice, the experts were therefore senior institute members. Despite evidence of increasing public relations activity in Asia through individual Australian practitioners, multinational corporations, and public relations consultancies, Australia–Asia trade, and the export of Australian public relations education, there is little evidence alterna-tive conceptualizations of public relations were informed by this regional or transnational activity. Focusing on conceptualizations of Asia in his-torical narratives of public relations reveals implicit assumptions in the construction of an Australian professional occupational identity. Asia–Australia interactions were marginal in the regulation and transmission of knowledge in relation to public relations education, until possibly the final decade of the twentieth century, and in historical accounts of the development of Australian public relations. Given the increased professionalization in the final decades of the twentieth century, it is worth noting that the professional occupational identity, with its focus on Australian experience, was increasingly exclusionary in terms of gender and national identity.

HISTORY AND HISTORIOGRAPHY

Rather than an evolutionary narrative of the development of Australian public relations, this book offers an alternative account. It does not claim to be a definitive history of Australian public relations in the second half of the twentieth century and recognizes that new histories will be constructed with access to new sources. Instead, this book interrogates existing historical narratives in that it considers public relations in terms of the industry's preoccupation with professional status and in the context of widespread changes in higher education, the Australian workforce and the global context. It has investigated links between the production of a public relations discourse and its broader social context and searched for shifts and disruptions in that discourse rather than linearity and progressivism (Foucault, 1972). This study has considered public relations from a broader societal and critical perspective, even as it drew on professional association archives and interviews with primarily PRIA members and former members. While the professional association's preoccupation with professional status and higher education reforms are not unique to Australia, embedding this study in a particular social and historical context allows a reconceptualization of public relations. This critical perspective is important in that it corrects inaccuracies in existing histories and identifies societal factors—external to PRIA and the public relations industry—that contributed in significant ways to the development of Australian public relations. These findings highlight the need both for more archival and evidentiary research into public relations and for more critical and reflexive approaches to researching public relations history, beyond the confines of the professional project.

This book does not offer an instrumentalist history designed to support claims for professional recognition, but rather an incomplete and dynamic account of how professional institutes sought to establish such recognition and claim social legitimacy. It recognizes history as a fluid process subject to new interpretations with new sources of evidence. Although this book corrects inaccuracies in widely accepted and uncritical historical accounts, it also offers a more nuanced, reflexive, and revisionist history in that it seeks to understand the social structures and ideologies that underpin conceptualizations of public relations. It therefore offers a critical history that allows history to "be a source of ongoing critique" (L'Etang, 2016, p. 29; see also Dean, 1994; Foucault, 1972; L'Etang, 1995). The privileging of particular historical narratives of Australian public relations has resulted in a narrow understanding that has ignored social contexts and limited theorizing of public relations.

The findings reported in this book highlight the need for critical reflection around public relations history and public relations historiography. Foregrounding questions about historical method and interpretation reveals the ideology informing the research design and construction of the historical narrative (L'Etang, 2015, 2016). This book located the researcher—as practitioner, educator, and scholar—to highlight their experiences in industry and in the academy and their links with the professional association. It identified a number of challenges of researching public relations history in Australia. These challenges included incomplete and geographically dispersed archives, some of which were studied for the first time. Rather than a single professional association, PRIA emerged from multiple, state-based professional institutes and "national" public relations journals in the twentieth century represented one or more states but rarely the whole nation. Given the dominance of practitioners' retrospective accounts, it is worth noting their remembered and reconstructed narratives tend to conform to the dominant paradigm and a professional discourse (Fitch, 2015). The dominant paradigm has thus framed understandings of public relations and its development in Australia and limited broader questions about its role in society and ignored links with other occupational fields.

This book problematizes the constitution of public relations history by challenging histories framed within a professional discourse, revealing attempts at occupational closure, and locating public relations within its social context. This interrogation of historical narratives therefore reveals new perspectives, such as the gendered and raced construction of professional occupational identities in Australia and the conceptualizations of public relations knowledge and expertise that played out in the higher education sector. These new perspectives contribute to a stronger understanding of the dynamic construction of "knowledge" and its significance for the professional project, including its constitution, its institutionalization, and attempts to regulate its transmission. PRIA's conceptualization of public relations knowledge late in the twentieth century drew on Australian industry experience, but framed within the dominant paradigm, and resulted in an increasingly narrow understanding of public relations and the role of education. The contested boundaries over the domain of public relations and the gendered stratification of different kinds of public relations activity reveal professional associations' struggle to establish public relations as a profession. Despite PRIA's successful claim to be the peak body in regulating education, the institute was unsuccessful in regulating or maintaining a clear jurisdiction over public relations activity in Australia. The competition between public relations and other fields, such as marketing, advertising, and organizational communication for intellectual and economic space (Abbott, 1988; Suddaby & Viale, 2011), points to an ongoing and significant struggle for the public relations industry in terms of establishing itself as a unique practice and gaining the professional recognition it has craved. These understandings, developed in response to specific social and political structures in earlier decades, continue to resonate in contemporary discourses of public relations.

Appendix A

Table 1 Schedule of Participant Interviews

Name	PRIA membership[a]	Date of interview
David Potts	FPRIA	December 4, 2010
Kevin Smith	FPRIA	January 18, 2011
Gae Synnott	FPRIA	March 23, 2011
Participant 4	FPRIA	March 25, 2011
Bill Mackey	FPRIA	March 30, 2011
Participant 6	FPRIA	August 12, 2011
Candy Tymson	FPRIA	August 18, 2011
Wendy Yorke	MPRIA	September 8, 2011
Participant 9	FPRIA	October 13, 2011
Participant 10	FPRIA	October 17, 2011
Marjorie Anderson	FPRIA	October 20, 2011
Steve Mackey	MPRIA	September 3, 2012
Jan Quarles	MPRIA	September 25, 2012
Peter Putnis	N/A	September 27, 2012

[a]Fellow (FPRIA) is a prestigious, invitation-only PRIA membership category introduced in 1987. It is offered to members who are considered by the national board to have made an outstanding contribution to the profession. MPRIA designates professional-grade membership. Recognition of membership level in this table does not necessarily signify that participants are current or active PRIA members.

© The Editor(s) (if applicable) and The Author(s) 2016
K. Fitch, *Professionalizing Public Relations*,
DOI 10.1057/978-1-137-57309-4

NOTE

1. In his interview, Potts stated in relation to university education that: "I don't want to be unkind to teaching staff but I think it's very necessary in our field to have been at the coalface in a responsible position and with a wide range of practice experience."

REFERENCES

1966 national convention programme. (1965, November/December). *Public Relations Journal*, p. 3.

Abbott, A. (1988). *The system of professions*. Chicago, IL: University of Chicago Press.

Academic qualification for public relations. (1955, April). Is it coming? A university professor's view. *P.R. News*, pp. 1–2.

Air news. (1954, August 19). *Balonne Beacon*, p. 5.

Airline girl will beat race planes. (1953, October 1). *The Newcastle Sun*, p. 18.

AJA interference threatens PR. (1993, June). *Public Relations: Official Journal of the Public Relations Institute of Australia (NSW)*, pp. 1–2.

AJA log of claims. (1992, May). *Public Relations: Official Journal of the Public Relations Institute of Australia (NSW)*, p. 1.

Alexander, D. (c. 1996). Marketing financial services to the multicultural market. *The PRofessional: Issues on Communication, Corporate Affairs and Public Relations*, *1*(3), 11.

Alexander, D. (2004). Changing the public relations curriculum: A new challenge for educators. *Prism*, *2*(1). Retrieved from www.prismjournal.org/number_2_1.html

All-climate wardrobe weighs only 66lb. (1954, February 19). *The Newcastle Sun*, p. 10.

Allert, J. (1990, April). A critical issue. *Profile: The Newsletter of the Public Relations Institute of Australia (WA)*, p. 3.

Amalgamation. (1953, July). *Pro-Files*, pp. 3–10.

Anderson, M. (1990, September). A bigger, brighter, more informative newsletter: Welcome to our inaugural first issue. *Public Relations: Official Journal of the New South Wales and Victorian Branches of the Public Relations Institute of Australia*, p. 1.

© The Editor(s) (if applicable) and The Author(s) 2016   129
K. Fitch, *Professionalizing Public Relations*,
DOI 10.1057/978-1-137-57309-4

Anderson, M. (1999). Public relations education in Australia. *Asia Pacific Public Relations Journal, 1*(1), 121–128.

Anthony, S. (2012). *Public relations and the making of modern Britain: Stephen Tallents and the birth of a progressive media profession.* Manchester, UK: Manchester University Press.

APBC offers first intermediate duration PR course. (1990, November). *Public Relations: Official Journal of the New South Wales and Victorian Branches of the Public Relations Institute of Australia,* p. 15.

Appointments. (1968, November/December). *Public Relations Australia,* p. 11.

Arrived on a visit, decided to stay. (1949, July 16). *News,* p. 11.

Ashcraft, K. L., Muhr, S. L., Rennstam, J., & Sullivan, K. (2012). Professionalization as a branding activity: Occupational identity and the dialectic of inclusivity-exclusivity. *Gender, Work & Organization, 19,* 467–488. doi:10.1111/j.1468-0432.2012.00600.x.

Assaf, J. (c. 1996). Communicating with diversity requires a diversity of communication. Public relations is the answer. *The PRofessional: Issues on Communication, Corporate Affairs and Public Relations, 1*(3), 8–10.

Australia's first PR knight. (1971, January/February). *Public Relations Australia,* pp. 8–9.

Australian Bureau of Statistics [ABS]. (1994, last updated May 9, 2006). *4102.0—Australian Social Trends, 1994.* Retrieved from http://www.abs.gov.au/AUSSTATS/abs@.nsf/2f762f95845417aeca25706c00834efa/e0a8b4f57a46da56ca2570ec007853c9!OpenDocument

Australian Women's Surfriders' Association. (1986). *Women in the surf.* South Melbourne, Australia: Educational Media Australia.

Berryman, R. (1996). Editor's note. *The PRofessional: Issues on Communication, Corporate Affairs and Public Relations* [Special Issue: Marketing Communication], *1*(4), 4.

Borland, H. (1995). Contested territories and evolving academic cultures: Whither communication studies? *Australian Journal of Communication, 22*(1), 14–30.

Breit, R., & Demetrious, K. (2010). Professionalisation and public relations: An ethical mismatch. *Ethical Space: The International Journal of Communication Ethics, 7*(4), 20–29.

British institute. (1953, February). *Pro-Files,* p. 3.

Burns, L. S. (2003). Reflections: Development of Australian journalism education. *Asia Pacific Media Educator, 14,* 57–75. Retrieved from http://ro.uow.edu.au/apme/vol1/iss14/5

Burson-Marsteller/Xinhua in China joint venture. (1985, October). *Profile: The Newsletter of the Public Relations Institute of Australia (WA),* p. 4.

Butler, B. (1998). Information subsidies, journalism routines and the Australian media: Market liberalization versus marketplace of ideas. *Prometheus: Critical Studies in Innovation, 16,* 27–45. doi:10.1080/08109029808629251.

Byrne, K. (2008). The value of academia: Variance among academic and practitioner perspectives on the role of public relations academics. *Asia Pacific Public Relations Journal, 9*, 17–34.

Can you help with the course? (1986, January). *Profile: The Newsletter of the Public Relations Institute of Australia (WA)*, p. 2.

Candidates sought for first accreditation exam. (1986, February/March). *Profile: The Newsletter of the Public Relations Institute of Australia (WA)*, p. 1.

Cantor, B., & Burger, C. (Eds.). (1984). *Experts in action: Inside public relations.* New York, NY: Longman.

Chay-Németh, C. (2009). Becoming professionals: A portrait of public relations in Singapore. In K. Sriramesh & D. Verčič (Eds.), *The global public relations handbook* (2nd ed., pp. 155–174). Abingdon, UK: Routledge.

Christensen, N. (2014, March 20). PR bosses: PR recruitment agencies and poorly trained uni graduates are a problem. *Mumbrella.* Retrieved from http://mumbrella.com.au/pr-bosses-recruitment-poorly-trained-uni-graduates-problem-215083

Colombo plan fellow. (1966, May). *Public Relations Journal*, p. 3.

Committee activities in brief: Tertiary liaison. (1990, July). *Profile: The Newsletter of the Public Relations Institute of Australia (WA)*, p. 3.

Corporates on the way up. (1996, November). *Public relations: The Newsletter of Public Relations Institute of Australia (NSW, VIC, QLD)*, p. 3.

Cover design. (1968, June/July). *Public Relations Australia*, p. 3.

Crable, R. E., & Vibbert, S. L. (1986). *Public relations as communication management.* Edina, MN: Bellwether Press.

Crawford, R. (2008). *But wait, there's more … A history of Australian advertising, 1900–2000.* Carlton, Australia: Melbourne University Press.

Crawford, R. (2015). A tale of two advertising cities: Sydney suits v. Melbourne creatives. *Journal of Australian Studies, 39*(2), 235–251. doi:10.1080/14443058.2015.1021706.

Crawford, R., & Dickenson, J. (2014). Advertising lives: Memoir and career. *History Australia, 11*(3), 134–156.

Crawford, R., & Macnamara, J. (2012). An "outside–in" PR history: Identifying the role of PR in history, culture and sociology. *Public Communication Review, 2*(1), 45–59. Retrieved from http://epress.lib.uts.edu.au/journals/index.php/pcr

Crawford, R., & Macnamara, J. (2014). An agent of change: Public relations in early-twentieth century Australia. In B. St John III, M. O. Lamme, & J. L'Etang (Eds.), *Pathways to public relations: Histories of practice and profession* (pp. 273–289), Abingdon, UK: Routledge.

Creedon, P. J. (1989). Public relations history misses "her story". *Journalism Educator, 44*(3), 26–30.

Curthoys, A. (1975). Towards a feminist labour history. In A. Curthoys, S. Eade, & P. Spearritt (Eds.), *Women at work* (pp. 88–95). Canberra, Australia: Australian Society for the Study of Labour History.

Curtin chatter. (1989, October). *Profile: The Newsletter of the Public Relations Institute of Australia (WA)*, p. 3.

Cutlip, S., & Center, A. H. (1971). *Effective public relations* (4th ed.). Englewood Cliffs, NJ: Prentice Hall.

Cutlip, S., Center, A. H., & Broom, G. M. (1985). *Effective public relations* (6th ed.). Englewood Cliffs, NJ: Prentice Hall.

Davies, C. (1996). The sociology of professions and the profession of gender. *Sociology, 30*, 661–678. doi:10.1177/0038038596030004003.

Davis, M. (2005). Profession and professionalism. In C. Mitcham (Ed.), *Encyclopedia of science, technology and ethics* (Vol. 3, pp. 1515–1519). Detroit, MI: Macmillan Reference USA.

Davis, A. (2013). *Promotional cultures*. Cambridge, UK: Polity.

De Bussy, N., & Wolf, K. (2009). The state of Australian public relations: Professionalisation and paradox. *Public Relations Review, 35*, 376–381. doi:10.1016/j.pubrev.2009.07.005.

Dean, M. (1994). *Critical and effective histories: Foucault's methods and historical sociology*. Abingdon, UK: Routledge.

Dell'oso, A-M. (1983, April 29). The psyche of selling: Public relations. *Australian Financial Review: Weekend Review*, pp. 29, 32.

Demetrious, K. (2013). *Public relations, activism, and social change: Speaking up*. London, UK: Routledge.

Demetrious, K. (2014). Surface effects: Public relations and the politics of gender. In C. Daymon & K. Demetrious (Eds.), *Gender and public relations: Critical perspectives on voice, image and identity* (pp. 20–45). Abingdon, UK: Routledge.

Dickenson, J. (2014). Global advertising histories: An Australian perspective. *History Compass, 12*(4), 321–332. doi:10.1111/hic3.12151.

Dickenson, J. (2016). *Australian women in advertising in the twentieth century*. Houndmills, UK: Palgrave Macmillan.

Dwyer, T. (Ed.). (1961). *The Australian public relations handbook*. Melbourne, Australia: Ruskin.

Editor, male or female. (1969, March/April). [Advertisement]. *Public Relations Australia*, p. 13.

Education venture's first financial return. (1992, February). *Public Relations: Official Journal for PRIA (NSW)*, pp. 1, 5.

Edwards, L. (2013). Institutional racism in cultural production: The case of public relations. *Popular Communication: The International Journal of Media and Culture, 11*(3), 242–256. doi:10.1080/15405702.2013.810084.

Edwards, L. (2014a). Discourse, credentialism and occupational closure in the communications industries: The case of public relations in the UK. *European Journal of Communication, 29*, 319–334. doi:10.1177/0267323113519228.

Edwards, L. (2014b). *Power, diversity and public relations*. London, UK: Routledge.

Edwards, L., & Hodges, C. (Eds.). (2011). *Public relations, society and culture: Theoretical and empirical explorations*. Abingdon, UK: Routledge.

Edwards, L., & Pieczka, M. (2013). Public relations and "its" media: Exploring the role of trade media in the enactment of public relations' professional project. *Public Relations Inquiry, 2*(1), 5–25. doi:10.1177/2046147X12464204.

Ellis, R. B., & Waller, D. S. (2011). Marketing education in Australia before 1965. *Australasian Marketing Journal, 19*, 115–121. doi:10.1016/j.ausmj.2011.03.003.

Eric White Associates [EWA]. (1966, October/November). [Advertisement]. *Public Relations Journal*, p. 16.

Etcetera. (1969, July/August). *Public Relations Australia*, p, 7.

Ewen, S. (1996). *PR! A social history of spin*. New York, NY: Basic Books.

Exam can be taken orally. (1990, May). *Profile: The Newsletter of the Public Relations Institute of Australia (WA)*, p. 2.

Expansion in India. (1993, May). *Public Relations: The Official Journal of PRIA (NSW) and PRIA (VIC)*, p. 11.

Factor, N. (1996). Adding people related skills to the marketing mix. *The PRofessional: Issues on communication, corporate affairs and public relations* [Special Issue: Marketing Communication], *1*(4), 11–12.

Fashion flight round the world. (1954, February 25). *The Sydney Morning Herald*, p. 4.

Faulconbridge, J., & Muzio, D. (2009). Legal education, globalization, and cultures of professional practice. *The Georgetown Journal of Legal Ethics, 22*, 1335–1359.

Fawsitt, J. (1954a, September 27). Expert's golden rules. *Sydney Morning Herald*, p. 3.

Fawsitt, J. (1954b, November 20). Hints and tips for travellers by air. *Queensland Times*, p. 3.

Fawsitt, J. (1954c, December 3). Complete wardrobe for a round-world air tour: Hints and tips for travellers. *Nambour Chronicle and North Coast Advertiser*, p. 3.

First PR accreditation exam planned for October. (1986, February/March). *Profile: The Newsletter of the Public Relations Institute of Australia (WA)*, p. 1.

Fisk, D. (1998a, February/March). The feminisation of PR—Just one trend shown from the survey. *Public Relations: Newsletter of PRIA (NSW) and PRIA (VIC)*, p. 1.

Fisk, D. (1998b, July/August). Will women be allowed to run PR? *Public Relations: Newsletter of Public Relations Institute of Australia (NSW, VIC, QLD)*, pp. 1–2.

Fitch, K. (2012). Industry perceptions of intercultural competence in Singapore and Perth. *Public Relations Review, 38*(4), 609–618. doi:10.1016/j.pubrev.2012.06.002.

Fitch, K. (2013). A disciplinary perspective: The internationalization of Australian public relations education. *Journal of Studies in International Education, 17*, 136–147. doi:10.1177/1028315312474898.

Fitch, K. (2013). A disciplinary perspective: The internationalization of Australian public relations education. *Journal of Studies in International Education, 17*(2), 136–147. doi:10.1177/1028315312474898 © 2013 Nuffic. Reprinted by Permission of SAGE Publications, Inc.

Fitch, K. (2014a). Professionalisation and public relations education: Industry accreditation of Australian university courses in the early 1990s. *Public Relations Review, 40*, 623–631. doi:10.1016/j.pubrev.2014.02.015.

Fitch, K. (2014b). Perceptions of Australian public relations education, 1985–1999. *Public Relations Inquiry, 3*, 271–291. doi:10.1177/2046147X14535398.

Fitch, K. (2015). Making history: Reflections on memory and "elite" interviews in public relations research. *Public Relations Inquiry, 4*(2), 131–144. doi:10.117 7/2046147X15580684.

Fitch, K. (2016a). Feminism and public relations. In J. L'Etang, D. McKie, N. Snow, & J. Xifra (Eds.), *Routledge handbook of critical public relations* (pp. 54–64). London, UK: Routledge.

Fitch, K. (2016b). Rethinking Australian public relations history in the mid-twentiethcentury.*Media International Australia, 160*.doi:10.1177/1329878X16651135

Fitch, K., & Surma, A. (2006). The challenges of international education: Developing a public relations unit for the Asian region. *Journal of University Learning and Teaching Practice, 2*(3), 104–113. Retrieved from http://ro. uow.edu.au/jutlp/vol3/iss2/4/

Fitch, K., & Third, A. (2010). Working girls: Revisiting the gendering of public relations. *Prism, 7*(4). Retrieved from http://www.prismjournal.org/fileadmin/Praxis/Files/Gender/Fitch_Third.pdf

Fitch, K., & Third, A. (2014). Ex-journos and promo girls: Feminization and professionalization in the Australian public relations industry. In C. Daymon & K. Demetrious (Eds.), Gender and public relations: Critical perspectives on voice, image and identity (pp. 247–267). Abingdon, UK: Routledge.

Fitch, K., & Third, A. (2014). Ex-journos and promo girls: Feminization and professionalization in the Australian public relations industry. In C. Daymon & K. Demetrious (Eds.), Gender and public relations: Critical perspectives on voice, image and identity (pp. 247–268). London, England: Routledge

Flew, T., Sternberg, J., & Adams, D. (2007). Revisiting the "media wars" debate. *Australian Journal of Communication, 34*(1), 1–27.

Flower, J. M. (2007). The birth and growth of an information agency. *Asia Pacific Public Relations Journal, 8*, 179–186.

Flower, T. (1988, September 13). Selecting the right PR consultant for the job. *Financial Review: AFR Survey (Public Relations)*, p. 64.

Fontana, A., & Frey, J. H. (2000). The interview: From structured questions to negotiated text. In N. K. Denzin & Y. S. Lincoln (Eds.), *Handbook of qualitative research* (2nd ed., pp. 645–672). Thousand Oaks, CA: Sage.

For your bookshelf. (1966, June). *Public Relations Journal*, p. 5.

Former PR man shipwrecked. (1955, April). *Pro-Files*, p. 9

Foucault, M. (1972). *The archaeology of knowledge & the discourse on language* (A. M. Sheridan Smith, Trans. 1971). London, UK: Tavistock Publications.

Free editorial publicity. (1955, April). *Pro-Files*, *2*(5), pp. 2–8.

Freidson, E. (1986). *Professional powers: A study of the institutionalization of formal knowledge*. Chicago, IL: University of Chicago Press.

Fröhlich, R., & Peters, S. B. (2007). PR bunnies caught in the agency ghetto? Gender stereotypes, organizational factors, and women's careers in PR agencies. *Journal of Public Relations Research, 19*, 229–254. doi:10.1080/10627260701331754.

Gae takes charge at WACAE. (1990, March). *Profile: The Newsletter of the Public Relations Institute of Australia (WA)*, p. 3.

Gallagher, M. (2011, April). *Envisioning the future global positioning of Australia in education, training and research*. Paper presented at the meeting of International Education Research Policy Symposium, Melbourne, Australia. Retrieved from http://www.lhmartininstitute.edu.au/documents/publications/gallagherenvisioningpaper.pdf

Give it to a busy woman. (1943, November 27). The Age, p. 8.

Gleeson, D. J. (2012). *Revisiting the foundations of public relations education in Australia*. Retrieved from Public Relations Institute of Australia [PRIA]. http://www.pria.com.au/priablog/revisiting-the-foundations-of-public-relations-education-in-australia

Gleeson, D. J. (2014). Public relations education in Australia, 1950–1975. *Journal of Communication Management, 18*, 193–206. doi:10.1108/JCOM-11-2012-0091.

Goetze, E. A. (1956, June). PR in London. *Pro-Files, 3*(1), pp. 17–18.

Gower, K. (2001). Rediscovering women in public relations: Women in the Public Relations Journal, 1945–1972. *Journalism History, 27*(1), 14–21.

Grand alliance for PR. (1953, September). *Pro-Files*, pp. 14–17.

Greenmount, L. (1990, February). The spotlight is focused on PR education courses. *Profile: The Newsletter of the Public Relations Institute of Australia (WA)*, p. 1.

Griffen-Foley, B. (2002). Political opinion polling and the professionalisation of public relations: Keith Murdoch, Robert Menzies, and the Liberal Party of Australia. *Australian Journalism Review, 24*(1), 41–59.

Griffen-Foley, B. (2003). A "Civilised Amateur": Edgar Holt and his life in letters and politics. *Australian Journal of Politics and History, 49*(1), 31–47.

Griffen-Foley, B. (2012). White, Eric (1915–1989). *Australian dictionary of biography*. Canberra, Australia: National Centre of Biography. Retrieved from http://adb.anu.edu.au/biography/white-eric-15809

Grunig, J. E. (2007, September). Vitae. Retrieved from http://comm.umd.edu/ sites/comm.umd.edu/files/JGrunigCV.pdf

Grunig, L. S. (2006, September). Larissa Schneider Grunig [CV]. Retrieved from http://comm.umd.edu/sites/comm.umd.edu/files/LGrunigCV2.pdf

Grunig, J., & Hunt, T. (1984). *Managing public relations.* New York, NY: Holt, Rinehart & Winston.

H&K Asia to be managed from Australia. (1990, November). *Public Relations: The Official Journal of PRIA (NSW) and PRIA (VIC),* p. 15.

Handfield, E. (1961a). The methods of public relations. In T. J. Dwyer (Ed.), *The Australian public relations handbook* (pp. 15–22). Melbourne, Australia: Ruskin Publishing.

Handfield, J. (1961b). Training for public relations. In T. J. Dwyer (Ed.), *The Australian public relations handbook* (pp. 210–219). Melbourne, Australia: Ruskin Publishing.

Handfield, E. (1974, October 30). Double bed and separate bank accounts. *The Australian Women's Weekly,* pp. 35, 37.

Handfield, E. (1976a). *Double bed and separate bank account.* Carlton, Australia: Platypus Press.

Handfield, E. (1976b, May 19). Are you ready to return to the workforce? A positive guide for women. *The Australian Women's Weekly,* pp. 30–31.

Hard times for IPR. (1967, March/April). *Public Relations Journal,* p. 7.

Harrison, K. (2011). *Strategic public relations: A practical guide to success.* South Yarra, Australia: Palgrave Macmillan.

Hatherell, W., & Bartlett, J. (2006). Positioning public relations as an academic discipline in Australia. *Asia Pacific Public Relations Journal, 6*(2), 1–13.

Haynes, K. (2012). Body beautiful? Gender, identity and the body in professional services firms. *Gender, Work & Organization, 19,* 489–507. doi:10.1111/ j.1468-0432.2011.00583.x.

Her job is air travel. (1954, September 8). *The Advertiser,* p. 20.

Her job is public relations. (1953, May 22). *The Advertiser,* p. 11.

Hickson, K. (2004). Ethical issues in practising public relations in Asia [Opinion]. *Journal of Communication Management, 8*(4), 345–353. doi:10.1108/ 13632540410807736.

High commission in a "selling speech." (1965, July/August). *Public Relations Journal,* p. 11.

Hill & Knowlton International. (1968). *Handbook on international public relations* (Vol. 2). New York, NY: Praeger.

Holstein, J., & Gubrium, J. (2008). Constructionist impulses in ethnographic fieldwork. In J. Holstein & J. Gubrium (Eds.), *Handbook of constructionist research* (pp. 373–395). New York, NY: Guildford Press.

Horne, L. (1989, July). Annual report 88/89. *Profile: The Newsletter of the Public Relations Institute of Australia (WA),* p. 4.

Horsley, S. J. (2009). Women's contributions to American public relations, 1940–1970. *Journal of Communication Management, 13,* 100–115. doi:10.1108/13632540910951731.

Hoy, P., Raaz, O., & Wehmeier, S. (2007). From facts to stories or from stories to facts? Analyzing public relations history in public relations textbooks. *Public Relations Review, 33,* 191–200. doi:10.1016/j.pubrev.2006.11.011.

Hutchinson, J. (1970). *Report on public relations activities, October 1970.* Perth, Australia: Public Works Department, Government of Western Australia.

Hydro-electric commission, Tasmania, has a vacancy for a publicity officer. (1968, February/March). [Advertisement]. *Public Relations Australia,* p. 19.

Ihlen, Ø., & van Ruler, B. (2009). Introduction: Applying social theory to public relations. In Ø. Ihlen, B. van Ruler, & M. Fredriksson (Eds.), *Public relations and social theory: Key figures and concepts* (pp. 1–20). New York, NY: Routledge.

Ihlen, Ø., & Verhoeven, P. (2009). Conclusions on the domain, context, concepts, issues and empirical avenues of public relations. In Ø. Ihlen, B. van Ruler, & M. Fredriksson (Eds.), *Public relations and social theory: Key figures and concepts* (pp. 323–340). New York, NY: Routledge.

Image Australia. (1966, October/November). [Advertisement]. *Public Relations Journal,* p. 16.

Interesting people. (1948, July 3). *The Australian Women's Weekly,* p. 10.

International P.R. association formed. (1955, August). *P.R. News,* p. 3.

International Public Relations Association [IPRA]. (1990, September). *Public relations education: Recommendations and standards* (Gold Paper No. 7). Report by the IPRA Education and Research Committee and the IPRA International Commission on Public Relations Education.

International Public Relations Association [IPRA]. (1994, November). *Public relations evaluation: Professional accountability* (Gold Paper No. 11). Geneva, Switzerland: Author.

International relations with Asia: Miss Elizabeth Palmer—Guest Speaker for November (1954, October/November). *Pro-Files, 2*(11), p. 2.

Jabara, L. (1986, September 16). Sound research, high standards vital ingredients for promotions. *Australian Financial Review: Public Relations,* p. 52.

Joe Joel, Film Executive. (1986, January 28). [Obituary]. *Sydney Morning Herald,* p. 5.

Johnston, J., & Macnamara, J. (2013). Public relations literature and scholarship in Australia: A brief history of change and diversification. *Prism, 10*(1). Retrieved from http://www.prismjournal.org/fileadmin/10_1/Johnston_Macnamara.pdf

Johnston, J., & Zawawi, C. (Eds.). (2000). *Public relations theory and practice.* St Leonards, Australia: Allen & Unwin.

June Dunstan takes on new WAIT PR course. (1986, February/March). *Profile: The Newsletter of the Public Relations Institute of Australia (WA),* p. 2.

Kaldor, A. G. (1967, July/August). The growth and nature of public relations in Australia. *Public Relations Journal*, pp. 1–8.

Kerr, G. F., Waller, D., & Patti, C. (2009). Advertising education in Australia: Looking back to the future. *Journal of Marketing Education, 31*, 264–274. doi:10.1177/0273475309345001.

King, M. T. (2012). Working with/in the archives. In S. Gunn & L. Faire (Eds.), *Research methods for history* (pp. 13–29). Edinburgh, UK: Edinburgh University Press.

Knight, N., & Heazle, M. (2011). *Understanding Australia's neighbours: An introduction to East and Southeast Asia* (2nd ed.). Port Melbourne, Australia: Cambridge University Press.

Kruckeberg, D. (1998). The future of PR education: Some recommendations. *Public Relations Review, 24*(2), 235–248. doi:10.1016/S0363-8111(99)80053-8.

Lamme, M. O. (2001). Furious desires and victorious careers: Doris E. Fleischman, counsel on public relations and advocate for working women. *American Journalism, 18*(3), 13–33. doi:10.1080/08821127.2001.10739322.

Lamme, M. O. (2007). Outside the prickly nest: Revisiting Doris Fleischman. *American Journalism, 24*(3), 85–107. doi:10.1080/08821127.2007.10678080.

Lamme, M., & Miller, K. (2010). Removing the spin: Toward a new theory of public relations history. *Journalism & Communication Monographs, 11*, 280–362. doi:10.1177/152263791001100402.

Larson, M. S. (1977). *The rise of professionalism: A sociological analysis*. Berkeley, CA: University of California Press.

Leffingwell, R. (1956, January/February). Public relations around the world. *P.R. News*, pp. 8–10.

Lerbinger in Australia. (1968). *Public Relations Australia*, p. 7.

Leroy-BOAC World Fashion Paradettes [Advertisement]. (1954, 6 September). *The Advertiser*, p. 13.

L'Etang, J. (1995, July). *Clio among the patriarchs? Historical and social scientific approaches to public relations: A methodological critique*. Paper presented at the meeting of the International Public Relations Symposium, Lake Bled, Slovenia.

L'Etang, J. (1999). Public relations education in Britain: An historical review in the context of professionalisation. *Public Relations Review, 25*(3), 261–289. doi:10.1016/S0363-8111(99)00019-3.

L'Etang, J. (2004). *Public relations in Britain: A history of professional practice in the 20th century*. Mahwah, NJ: Lawrence Erlbaum.

L'Etang, J. (2008a). *Public relations: Concepts, practice and critique*. London, UK: Sage.

L'Etang, J. (2008b). Writing PR history: Issues, methods and politics. *Journal of Communication Management, 12*(4), 319–335. doi:10.1108/13632540810919783.

L'Etang, J. (2009). "Radical PR"—Catalyst for change or an aporia? *Ethical Space: The International Journal of Communication Ethics, 6*(2), 13–18. Retrieved from http://www.communicationethics.net/journal/v6n2/v6n2_feat1.pdf

L'Etang, J. (2014). Public relations and historical sociology: Historiography as reflexive critique. *Public Relations Review, 40*(4), 654–660. doi:10.1016/j.pubrev.2013.12.009.

L'Etang, J. (2015a). What is public relations historiography? Philosophy of history, historiography and public relations. In T. Watson (Ed.), *Perspectives on public relations historiography and historical theorization* (pp. 69–84). Houndmills, UK: Palgrave Macmillan.

L'Etang, J. (2015b). "It's always been a sexless trade"; "It's clean work"; "There's very little velvet curtain": Gender and public relations in post-Second World War Britain. *Journal of Communication Management, 19*(4), 354–370. doi:10.1108/JCOM-01-2014-0006.

L'Etang, J. (2016). History as a source of critique: Historicity and knowledge, societal change, activism and movements. In J. L'Etang, D. McKie, N. Snow, & J. Xifra (Eds.), *Routledge handbook of critical public relations* (pp. 28–40). London, UK: Routledge.

Lewis, G. (1982). The Anglo-American influence on Australian communication education. *Australian Journal of Communication, 1&2*, 14–20.

IPR London. (1956, June). *Pro-Files, 3*(1), p. 4.

Macdonald, K. (1995). *The sociology of the professions.* London, UK: Sage.

MacIntosh, I. (1986, September 16). Professionalism heralds new era. *Australian Financial Review: Public Relations*, p. 45.

Mackey, B. (1989, December). Looking back on a dramatic decade. *Profile: The Newsletter of the Public Relations Institute of Australia (WA)*, p. 3.

Macnamara, J. (1984). *Public relations handbook for managers and executives.* Melbourne, Australia: Margaret Gee Media.

Macnamara, J. (1992). *The Asia Pacific public relations handbook.* Lindfield, Australia: Archipelago Press.

Macnamara, J. (1996). *Public relations handbook for managers and executives* (Rev. ed.). Melbourne, Australia: Prentice Hall Australia.

Macnamara, J. (2000). *Jim Macnamara's public relations handbook.* Melbourne, Australia: Information Australia.

Macnamara, J., & Crawford, R. (2010a). Reconceptualising public relations in Australia: A historical and social re-analysis. *Asia Pacific Public Relations Journal, 11*(2), 17–33.

Macnamara, J., & Crawford, R. (2010b). Editorial. *Public Communication Review, 1*(1), 1–2. Retrieved from http://epress.lib.uts.edu.au/journals/index.php/pcr/article/view/1429/1527

Macnamara, J., & Crawford, R. (2014). Public relations. In B. Griffen-Foley (Ed.), *A companion to the Australian media* (pp. 374–377). North Melbourne, Australia: Australian Scholarly Publishing.

Madden, J. (1973, July 11). The can people—BHP can fraud detailed. *Woroni*, pp. 4–12.

Major plans to strengthen the institute. (1984, September). *Profile: The Newsletter of the Public Relations Institute of Australia (WA)*, p. 3.

Maras, S. (2003). Presidents reflect on ANZCA: Past and future. *Australian Journal of Communication, 30*(1), 1–24.

Maras, S. (2004). Thinking about the history of ANZCA: An Australian perspective. *Australian Journal of Communication, 31*(2), 13–51.

Maras, S. (2006). The emergence of communication studies in Australia as "curriculum idea". *Australian Journal of Communication, 33*(2,3), 43–62.

Marginson, S., & Considine, M. (2000). *The enterprise university: Power, governance and reinvention in Australia*. Cambridge, UK: Cambridge University Press.

Mathews, I. (1984). *How to use the media in Australia* (2nd ed.). Melbourne, Australia: Margaret Gee Media.

McCallum, B. (1978). *Tales untold: Memoirs of an ABC publicity officer*. Melbourne, Australia: Hawthorn Press.

McIndoe, L. (1970, February/March). Communication is easy, or is it? *Public Relations Australia*, p. 11.

McKie, D. (2012). Textbook publishing: Opportunism, theory, and the captive audience. *Public Relations Inquiry, 1*, 107–110. doi:10.1177/2046147X11422649.

McKie, D., & Hunt, M. (1999). Staking claims: Marketing, public relations and territories. *Asia Pacific Public Relations Journal, 1*(2), 43–58.

McKie, D., & Munshi, D. (2007). *Reconfiguring public relations: Ecology, equity and enterprise*. Abingdon, UK: Routledge.

Meet the members. (1956, July/August). *P.R. News, 2*(5), pp. 5–6.

Membership. (1955, November–December). *P.R. News*, pp. 12–15.

Miller, K. (1999). *The voice of business: Hill & Knowlton and postwar public relations*. Chapel Hill, NC: University of North Carolina Press.

Miller, K. (2000). Public relations history: Knowledge and limitations. In M. E. Roloff (Ed.), *Communication yearbook 23* (2012th ed., pp. 381–420). New York, UK: Routledge.

Miller, K. S. (1997). Woman, man, lady, horse: Jane Stewart, public relations executive. *Public Relations Review, 23*, 249–269. doi:10.1016/S0363-8111(97)90035-7.

Mina, J. (1996, July). Breaking the glass ceiling. *Public Relations: The Newsletter of the Public Relations Institute of Australia (NSW, VIC, QLD)*, pp. 6–7.

Mission to China. (1996, November). *Public Relations: The Newsletter of the Public Relations Institute of Australia (NSW, VIC, QLD)*, p. 1.

Mojo Corporate opens in Perth. (1986, July). *Campaign Brief* [page unknown].

Molloy, B., & Lennie, J. (1990). *Communication studies in Australia: A statistical study of teachers, students, and courses in Australian tertiary institutions* (Policy and research report No. 1). Brisbane, Australia: The Communication Centre, Queensland University of Technology.

Morath, K. (2008). *Pride and prejudice: Conversations with Australia's public relations legends*. Elanora, Australia: Nuhouse Press.

Morton-Evans, M. (1996, October). Grave doubts about overseas PRs. *Public Relations: The Newsletter of the Public Relations Institute of Australia (NSW, VIC, QLD)*, p. 9.

Motion, J., & Weaver, C. K. (2005). A discourse perspective for critical public relations research: Life Sciences Network and the battle for truth. *Journal of Public Relations Research, 17*, 49–67. doi:10.1207/s1532754xjprr1701_5.

Munshi, D., & Edwards, L. (2011). Understanding "race" in/and public relations: Where do we start and where should we go? *Journal of Public Relations Research, 23*(4), 349–367. doi:10.1080/1062726X.2011.605976.

Muzio, D., & Kirkpatrick, I. (2011). Introduction: Professions and organizations—A conceptual framework. *Current Sociology, 59*, 389–405. doi:10.1177/0011392111402584.

Myers, H. (1976). Public relations and the future. In J. D. S. Potts (Ed.), *Public relations practice in Australia* (pp. 323–331). Sydney, Australia: McGraw-Hill.

Myers, C. (2014). Reconsidering the corporate narrative in U.S. PR history: A critique of Alfred Chandler's influence on PR historiography. *Public Relations Review, 40*(4), 676–683. doi:10.1016/j.pubrev.2014.02.021.

National convention in Sydney next April. (1968, April/May). *Public Relations Australia*, p. 1.

National council accredits Western Australia's public relations course. (1984, December). *Profile: The Newsletter of the Public Relations Institute of Australia (WA)*, p. 1.

National journal, 1990 report of the PRIA. (1990, November). *Public relations: Official Journal of the New South Wales and Victorian Branches of the Public Relations Institute of Australia*, p. 4.

National P.R. institute. (1956, September/October). *P.R. News*, p. 8.

New appointments. (1968, February/March). *Public Relations Australia*, p. 7.

New breed of P.R. man. (1967, March/April). *Public Relations Journal*, p. 1.

New faces at IPR. (1989, September). *Profile: The Newsletter of the Public Relations Institute of Australia (WA)*, p. 3.

New members. (1956, July). *Pro-Files, 4*(2), p. 5.

New Tas. council. (1970, November/December). *Public Relations Australia*, p. 7.

New W.A. chapter. (1971, January/February). *Public Relations Australia*, p. 3.

Nicholls, F. (2007). John Matthew Flower [Obituary]. *Asia Pacific Public Relations Journal, 8*, 187–188.

Noordegraaf, M. (2011). Remaking professionals? How associations and professional education connect professionalism and organizations. *Current Sociology, 59*, 465–488. doi:10.1177/0011392111402716.

NSW approach us on federal body. (c. 1953). *Pro-Files, 1*(3), pp. 1–5.

NSW course in public relations. (1965, September/October). *Public Relations Journal*, p. 3.

NSW formal luncheon. (1965, May/June). *Public Relations Journal*, p. 2.

NSW's "Man of Achievement." (1970, November/December). *Public Relations Australia*, p. 5.

Odd thoughts on PR. (1952, October). *Pro-Files*, p. 4.

One world of fashion. (1959). [Programme, International Trade Fair, Exhibition Building, Melbourne, 26 February–14 March]. Melbourne, Australia: John and Esta Handfield (Public Relations).

Oral examination, 1990 report of the PRIA. (1990, November). *Public Relations: Official Journal of the New South Wales and Victorian Branches of the Public Relations Institute of Australia*, p. 3.

Organiser for Rachel Forster Hospital: Miss B. Hoyles appointed. (1940, July 18). *Sydney Morning Herald*, p. 14.

Outline of the Mitchell College P.R. course. (1971, June/July). *Public Relations Australia*, pp. 10–11.

Parliament of NSW. (n. d.). Sir Asher Alexander JOEL, K.B.E (1912–1998). Retrieved from http://www.parliament.nsw.gov.au/prod/PARLMENT/members.nsf/ec78138918334ce3ca256ea200077f5d/7332d0470aac4794ca256e7f001192be!OpenDocument

Patterson, H. E. (1952). New P.R. lecture course proposed [Letter to the editor]. *Pro-File, 1*(2), pp. 3–4.

Pearson, R. (2009). Perspectives on public relations history. In R. Heath, E. L. Toth, & D. Waymer (Eds.), *Rhetorical and critical approaches to public relations II* (pp. 92–109). New York, NY: Routledge.

Personal. (1952). *Pro-Files, 1*(3), p. 6.

Personal. (1953, March). *Pro-Files, 1*(5), p. 5.

Petelin, R. (2005). Editing from the edge: De-territorializing public relations scholarship. *Public Relations Review, 31*, 458–462. doi:10.1016/j.pubrev.2005.08.002.

Pieczka, M. (2000). Objectives and evaluation in public relations work: What do they tell us about expertise and professionalism? *Journal of Public Relations Research, 12*(3), 211–233. doi:10.1207/S1532754XJPRR1203_1.

Pieczka, M. (2002). Public relations expertise deconstructed. *Media Culture Society, 24*(3), 301–323. doi:10.1177/016344370202400302.

Pieczka, M. (2006). Paradigms, systems theory and public relations. In J. L'Etang & M. Pieczka (Eds.), *Public relations: Critical debates and contemporary practice* (pp. 333–357). Mahwah, NJ: Lawrence Erlbaum.

Pieczka, M. (2007). Case studies as narrative accounts of public relations practice. *JournalofPublicRelationsResearch,19*,333–356.doi:10.1080/10627260701402432.

Pieczka, M., & L'Etang, J. (2006). Public relations and the question of professionalism. In J. L'Etang & M. Pieczka (Eds.), *Public relations: Critical debates and contemporary practice* (pp. 265–278). Mahwah, NJ: Lawrence Erlbaum.

Planning in hand for 1988 IPRA congress in Australia. (1985, May). *Profile: The Newsletter of the Public Relations Institute of Australia* (WA), p. 1.

Plater, R. (1976). Public relations in Australia: Introduction by the National President of the Public Relations Institute of Australia. In J. D. S. Potts (Ed.), *Public relations practice in Australia* (p. iv). Sydney, Australia: McGraw Hill.

Potts, J. D. S. (Ed.). (1976). *Public relations practice in Australia*. Sydney, Australia: McGraw Hill.

Potts, J. D. S. (1986, September 16). Courses satisfy demand for broader professional skills. *Australian Financial Review: Public Relations*, p. 50.

Potts, J. D. S. (2008, November). *Evening with a Fellow*. Paper presented at the meeting of Public Relations Institute of Australia, Sydney, Australia. Retrieved from www.pria.com.au/resources//an-evening-with-a-fellow-david-potts-november-2008

PR education: Graduate perceptions. (1997, May). *Profile*, p. 5.

PR in the jungle. (1955, April). *P.R. News*, p. 5.

PR industry at the crossroads: Results announced for first-ever survey of P.R. industry. (1985, October). *Profile: The Newsletter of the Public Relations Institute of Australia* (WA), pp. 1–2.

PR job in Fiji. (1955). *Pro-Files*, pp. 7–8.

PR masters degree in Queensland. (1984, December). *Profile: The Newsletter of the Public Relations Institute of Australia* (WA), p. 1.

PRIA membership list. (1968, April/May). *Public Relations Australia* [Supplement], pp. i–xii.

PRIA national convention an outstanding success. (1990, November). *Public Relations: Official Journal of the New South Wales and Victorian Branches of the PRIA*, p. 5.

PRIA (NSW) to run PR courses in Sydney. (1990, February). *Public Relations: An Official Journal of the Public Relations Institute of Australia (NSW)*, pp. 1–2.

Pritchett, J. (1988, September 13). Future for PR consultants: Giants and pygmies needed. *Australian Financial Review: AFR Survey (Public Relations)*, p. 62.

Profile: Noel Griffiths. (1965, July/August). *Public Relations Journal*, pp. 6–7.

Programme, Public Relations National Convention. (1971, August/September). *Public Relations Australia* [Supplement between pp. 6–7].

Public relations course starts at WAIT in 1986. (1986, January). *Profile: The Newsletter of the Public Relations Institute of Australia* (WA), p. 2.

Public relations education. (1966, March). *Public Relations Journal*, p. 21.

Public relations growth in Japan. (1966, January/February). *Public Relations Journal*, pp. 8–9.

Public relations in a shrinking world. (1966, March). [Conference program]. *Public Relations Journal*, pp. 18–19.

Public Relations Institute of Australia [PRIA]. (1964). *Public relations in a changing world by Don Barnes, Esta Handfield*. Conference proceedings, National Convention of Public Relations Institute of Australia, Sydney, Australia.

Public Relations Institute of Australia [PRIA]. (1991). *Guidelines for the accreditation of public relations courses at Australian tertiary institutions*. Sydney, Australia: Public Relations Institute of Australia.

Public Relations Institute of Australia [PRIA]. (1996). *Guidelines for the accreditation of public relations courses at Australian tertiary institutions*. Sydney, Australia: Public Relations Institute of Australia.

Public Relations Institute of Australia [PRIA]. (2007). Kevin Smith Testimonial Lunch. Retrieved from http://www.pria.com.au/sitebuilder/events/events/files/48816/priawakevinsmithtestimoniallunchregistration.pdf

Public Relations Institute of Australia [PRIA]. (2010). Sir Asher Joel. Retrieved from http://www.pria.com.au/aboutus/in-honour/sir-asher-joel

Public Relations Institute of Australia [PRIA]. (2012). David Potts FPRIA OAM recognized in Australia Day Honours List. Retrieved from http://www.pria.com.au/priablog/david-potts-fpria-oam-recognized-in-australia-day-honours-list

Public relations luncheon. (1950, December 12). *The West Australian*, p. 20.

Public relations officer. (1941, January 30). *The Argus*, p. 8.

Putnis, P. (1986). Communication studies in Australia: Paradigms and contexts. *Media Culture Society, 8*, 143–157.

Putnis, P. (1988). The communication curriculum: Educating communication practitioners. *Australian Communication Review, 9*(2), 29–44.

Putnis, P. (1993). National preoccupations and international perspectives in communication studies in Australia. *The Electronic Journal of Communication, 3*(3&4). Retrieved from http://www.cios.org/EJCPUBLIC/003/3/00333.HTML

Putnis, P., & Axford, B. (2002). Communication and media studies in Australian universities: Diverse, innovative and isomorphic. *Australian Journal of Communication, 29*(1), 1–20.

Quarles, J. (1993). Up from down under: Public relations education in Australia. *International Public Relations Review, 16*(4), 21–24.

Quarles, J., & Potts, D. (1990, September). Public relations education in Australia: A report prepared for the National Executive of the Public Relations Institute of Australia. Sydney, Australia: Public Relations Institute of Australia.

Quarles, J., & Rowlings, B. (1993). *Practising public relations: A case study approach*. Melbourne, Australia: Longman Cheshire.

Raciti, M. (2010). Marketing Australian higher education at the turn of the 21st century: A précis of reforms, commercialisation and the new university hierarchy. *e–Journal of Business Education & Scholarship of Teaching*, 4(1), 32–41. Retrieved from http://www.ejbest.org/Volume4-Issue1.html

Ray, G. (1990, November). A landmark newsletter. *Public Relations: Official Journal of the New South Wales and Victorian Branches of the Public Relations Institute of Australia*, p. 1.

Ray, G. (1991, March). Public relations institute to accredit education programs. *Public Relations: Official Journal of the New South Wales and Victorian Branches of the Public Relations Institute of Australia*, pp. 1–2.

Rea, J. (2002, July). *The feminisation of public relations: What's in it for the girls?* Paper presented at the meeting of Australia and New Zealand Communication Association, Gold Coast, Queensland. Retrieved from http://www.anzca.net/conferences/conference-papers/41-adam.html

Read, K. A. H. (1956, May/June). The Ceylon tea industry & P.R. *P.R. News*, pp. 12–14.

Rebeiro, D. (1997, August). The role of PR in China. *Profile: The Newsletter of the Public Relations Institute of Australia (WA)*, p. 3.

Reed, M. (1996). Expert power and control in late modernity: An empirical review and theoretical synthesis. *Organization Studies, 17*, 573–597. doi:10.1177/017084069601700402.

Report on education. (1990, October). *Public Relations: Official Journal of the New South Wales and Victorian Branches of the Public Relations Institute of Australia*, p. 4.

Reproduced by permission of Elsevier from Fitch, K. (2014). Professionalisation and public relations education: Industry accreditation of Australian university courses in the early 1990s. *Public Relations Review, 40*, 623–631. doi:10.1016/j.pubrev.2014.02.015.

Reproduced by permission of SAGE Publications Ltd., London, Los Angeles, New Delhi, Singapore and Washington DC, from Fitch, K. (2015). *Making history: Reflections on memory and "elite" interviews in public relations research. Public Relations Inquiry, 4*(2), 131–144. doi:10.1177/2046147X15580684. (© The Author, 2015)

Reproduced by permission of SAGE Publications Ltd., London, Los Angeles, New Delhi, Singapore and Washington DC, from Fitch, K. (2014). Perceptions of public relations education, 1985–1999. *Public Relations Inquiry, 3*(3), 271–291. doi:10.1177/2046147X14535398. (© The Author, 2014)Roper, J. (2005). Symmetrical communication: Excellent public relations or a strategy for hegemony? *Journal of Public Relations Research, 17*, 69–86. doi:10.1207/s1532754xjprr1701_6.

Rush sets up in Hong Kong. (1989, October). *Profile: The Newsletter of the Public Relations Institute of Australia (WA)*, p. 4.

Rutzou, D. (2010, September 1). Enthusiasm for public relations [Blog post]. *PR Blog: Dennis Rutzou Public Relations*. Retrieved from http://www.drpr.com.au/public-relations-blog/2010/09/01/enthusiasm-for-public-relations/

S.A. course in public relations. (1965, November/December). *Public Relations Journal*, p. 2.

Sefiani, R. (c. 1996). Communicating in multicultural Asia. *The PRofessional: Issues on Communication, Corporate Affairs and Public Relations, 1*(3), 12–14.

Serle, G. (2000). Medley, Sir John Dudley Gibbs (Jack) (1891–1962). *Australian dictionary of biography*. Canberra, Australia: Australian National University. Retrieved from http://adb.anu.edu.au/biography/medley-sir-john-dudley-gibbs-jack-11101/text19763

Sha, B-L. (2011, March 8). PR women: New data show gender-based salary gap is widening. *Ragan's PR Daily*. Retrieved from http://www.prdaily.com/Main/Articles/PR_women_New_data_show_genderbased_salary_gap_is_w_7468.aspx

Sheehan, M. (2007, November). *Australian public relations campaigns: A select historical perspective 1899–1950*. Paper presented at the meeting of Australian media traditions: Distance and diversity: Reaching new audiences. Bathurst, Australia. Retrieved from http://www.csu.edu.au/special/amt/publication/sheehan.pdf

Sheehan, M. (2010). Eric White. Retrieved from Public Relations Institute of Australia [PRIA]. www.pria.com.au/aboutus/in–honour–2/eric–white

Sheehan, M. (2014a). Foundations of public relations in Australia and New Zealand. In J. Johnston & M. Sheehan (Eds.), *Public relations: Theory and practice* (4th ed., pp. 20–47). Crows Nest, Australia: Allen & Unwin.

Sheehan, M. (2014b). Australasia. In T. Watson (Ed.), *Asian perspectives on the development of public relations: Other voices* (pp. 4–13). Houndmills, UK: Palgrave Macmillan.

Sherman, B., & Griffin, J. (1976). Public relations administration. In J. D. S. Potts (Ed.), *Public relations practice in Australia* (pp. 77–86). Sydney, Australia: McGraw Hill.

Sinclair, J. (1991). The advertising industry in Australia: Globalisation and national culture. *Media Information Australia, 62*, 31–40.

Sinclair, J. (2014). Advertising agencies. In B. Griffen-Foley (Ed.), *A companion to the Australian media* (pp. 6–7). North Melbourne, Australia: Australian Scholarly Publishing.

Sparrow, M. (1956, January/February). What we're doing and saying. *P.R. News*, pp. 4–6.

Sparrow, M., & Fawsitt, J. (1956, May/June). What we're doing and saying. *P.R. News*, pp. 7–11.

Special PRIA state conference 1996 edition. (1996, September). *Profile*, pp. 1, 4.

Sriramesh, K. (Ed.). (2004). *Public relations in Asia: An anthology*. Singapore, Singapore: Thomson Learning.

St John III, B., Lamme, M. O., & L'Etang, J. (Eds.). (2014). Introduction: Realizing new pathways to public relations history. In B. St John III, M. O.

Lamme & J. L'Etang (Eds.), *Pathways to public relations: Histories of practice and profession* (pp. 1–8). Abingdon, UK: Routledge.

Stanger, J. (1965a, March/April). People in public relations. *Public Relations Journal*, p. 10.

Stanger, J. (1965b, November/December). People in public relations. *Public Relations Journal*, pp. 4–5.

Stanger, J. (1966, January/February). People in public relations. *Public Relations Journal*, p. 4.

Stanley, D. (1985). *Finding Fiji.* Chico, CA: Moon Publications.

Starck, N. (1999). *Accredited or discredited? A qualitative study of public relations education at Australian universities.* Unpublished master's thesis, RMIT, Melbourne, Australia.

State conference and Grunig visit: Highlights of exciting programme. (1996, May). *Profile*, p. 8.

Steedman, C. (2002). *Dust: The archive and cultural history.* New Brunswick, NJ: Rutgers University Press.

Student workshop gains wide industry support. (1989, October). *Profile: The Newsletter of the Public Relations Institute of Australia (WA)*, p. 2.

Suddaby, R., & Viale, T. (2011). Professionals and field-level change: Institutional work and the professional project. *Current Sociology, 59*, 423–442. doi:10.1177/0011392111402586.

Talkabout. (1954, June 22). *The Argus*, p. 6.

Tansey, O. (2007). Process tracing and elite interviewing: A case for non-probability sampling. *PS: Political Science and Politics, 40*, 765–772. doi:10.1017/S1049096507071211.

Tasmania at last. (1967, March/April). *Public Relations Journal*, p. 3.

Tasmanian secretary. (1969, March/April). *Public Relations Australia*, p. 13.

That list. (1956, July). *Pro-Files*, pp. 6–7.

The first public relations convention ever held in Australia. (1954, April). *Pro-Files, 2*(6), pp. 2–3.

The most powerful man. (2002, January 21). *Crikey.* Retrieved from http://www.crikey.com.au/2002/01/21/the-most-powerful-pr-man-of-all/

The professional challenge. (1989, October). *Profile: The Newsletter of the Public Relations Institute of Australia (WA)*, p. 3.

The speakers. (1966, March). Public relations in a shrinking world: March 10–13. *Public Relations Journal*, pp. 11–17.

The weekly round. (1959, June 3). *The Australian Women's Weekly*, p. 2.

Third national public relations convention. (1969, March/April). Public relations: Performance and prospects [Convention theme]. *Public Relations Australia* [4-page supplement].

Thomson, A. (2012). Life stories and historical analysis. In S. Gunn & L. Faire (Eds.), *Research methods for history* (pp. 101–117). Edinburgh, UK: Edinburgh University Press.

Thomson, I. (1956, May/June). Meet the members: No. 2—Asher Alexander Joel OBE. *P.R. News*, pp. 3–6.

To the editor. (1966, July). *Public Relations Journal*, p. 11.

Top marks for state convention. (1989, October). *Profile: The Newsletter of the Public Relations Institute of Australia (WA)*, p. 1.

Top offers for top youngsters. (1989, October). *Profile: The Newsletter of the Public Relations Institute of Australia (WA)*, p. 2.

Training in S.A. (1967, March/April). *Public Relations Journal*, p. 7.

Traveller to display wardrobe. (1954, August 13). *The Newcastle Sun*, p. 12.

Trusler, C. (1966, January/February). The film as a public relations medium. *Public Relations Journal*, pp. 8–9.

Turnbull, N. (2010). *How PR works—But often doesn't*. Melbourne, Australia: N. S. & J. S. Turnbull. Retrieved from http://noelturnbull.com/wp-content/uploads/2010/06/How-PR-works-but-often-doesnt.pdf

Turner, G. (2002). Public relations. In S. Cunningham & G. Turner (Eds.), *The media and communications in Australia* (pp. 217–225). Crows Nest, Australia: Allen & Unwin.

Turner, G., Bonner, F., & Marshall, P. D. (2000). *Fame games: The production of celebrity in Australia*. Cambridge, NY: Cambridge University Press.

Tymson, C., Lazar, P., & Lazar, R. (2008). *The new Australian and New Zealand public relations manual* (5th ed.). Manly, Australia: Tymson Communications.

Tymson, C., & Sherman, B. (1987). *The Australian public relations manual*. Sydney, Australia: Millennium Books.

UK suspensions. (1967, March/April). *Public Relations Journal*, p. 3.

van Ruler, B. (2005). Professionals are from Venus, scholars are from Mars [Commentary]. *Public Relations Review, 31*, 159–173. doi:10.1016/j.pubrev.2005.02.022.

Vic. membership. (1970, February/March). *Public Relations Australia*, p. 6.

Victory in WA (1967, September/October). *Public Relations Journal*, p. 11.

Visitors add value to WA. (1997, November/December). *Profile*, p. 5.

WA state council concerned at national accreditation plans. (1985, February). *Profile: The Newsletter of the Public Relations Institute of Australia (WA)*, p. 2.

Walker, D., & Sobocinska, A. (Eds.). (2012). *Australia's Asia: From yellow peril to Asian century*. Perth, Australia: UWA Publishing.

Walker, G. (1991, Spring). From the editor [Editorial]. *Public Relations Educators Association of Australia Newsletter*, p. 8.

Walkington, J., & Vanderheide, R. (2008, July 1–4). *Enhancing the pivotal roles in workplace learning and community engagement through transdisciplinary "cross talking."* Paper presented at the meeting of HERDSA International Conference: Engaging Communities, Rotorua, New Zealand. Retrieved from http://www.herdsa.org.au/wp-content/uploads/conference/2008/papers/Walkington.pdf

Ward, I. (1999). The early use of radio for political communication in Australia and Canada: John Henry Austral, Mr Sage and the Man from Mars. *Australian Journal of Politics & History, 45*, 311–330. doi:10.1111/1467-8497.00067.

Ward, I. (2003). An Australian PR state? *Australian Journal of Communication, 30*(1), 25–42.

Watson, T. (2011). Archive of the International Public Relations Association. Bournemouth, England: The Media School, Bournemouth University. Retrieved from http://microsites.bournemouth.ac.uk/historyofpr/files/2011/11/IPRA-ARCHIVE.pdf

Watson, T. (2013, June). *The scholarship of public relations history: A report card* [Keynote address]. Paper presented at the meeting of International History of Public Relations Conference, Bournemouth, England. Retrieved from http://microsites.bournemouth.ac.uk/historyofpr/files/2010/11/Tom-Watson-IHPRC-2013-Keynote-Address4.pdf

Watson, T. (Ed.). (2014–2015). National perspectives on the development of public relations: Other voices. Houndsmills, UK: Palgrave Macmillan.

Watson, T. (2015). What in the world is public relations? In T. Watson (Ed.), *Perspectives on public relations historiography and historical theorization* (pp. 4–19). Houndmills, UK: Palgrave Macmillan.

Watson, T., & Macnamara, J. (2013). The rise and fall of IPRA in Australia: 1959 to 2000. *Asia Pacific Public Relations Journal.* Retrieved from http://eprints.bournemouth.ac.uk/21225/

We'll soon be British. (1952, October). *Pro-Files*, pp. 1–2.

Weaver, C. K. (2016). Who's afraid of the big bad wolf? Critical public relations as a cure for media studies' fear of the dark. In J. L'Etang, D. McKie, N. Snow, & J. Xifra (Eds.), *The Routledge handbook of critical public relations* (pp. 260–273). Abingdon, UK: Routledge.

Welcome to eight new members. (1984, September). *Profile: The Newsletter of the Public Relations Institute of Australia (WA)*, p. 3.

What we're doing and saying. (1955, November–December). *P.R. News*, p. 20.

What we're doing and saying. (1956, March/April). *P.R. News*, p. 6.

Wide scope for public relations. (1951, June 15). *The Advertiser*, p. 13.

Williams, M. (1996). Public relationship marketing. *The PRofessional: Issues on Communication, Corporate Affairs and Public Relations* [Special Issue: Marketing Communication], *1*(4), pp. 13–15.

Witz, A. (1992). *Professions and patriarchy.* London, UK: Routledge.

Wolf, K., & De Bussy, N. (2008). Perceptions of professionalism: Practitioner reflections on the state of Australian public relations. *Asia Pacific Public Relations Journal, 9*, 4–16.

Wool wings its way around the world. (1959, June 3). *The Australian Women's Weekly*, p. 11.

Wright, D. (2011). History and development of public relations education in North America: A critical analysis. *Journal of Communication Management, 15,* 236–255. doi:10.1108/13632541111151005.

Yaxley, H. M. L. (2013). Career experiences of women in British public relations (1970–1989). *Public Relations Review, 39*(2), 156–165. doi:10.1016/j.pubrev.2013.03.009.

Zawawi, C. (2009). A history of public relations in Australia. In J. Johnston & C. Zawawi (Eds.), *Public relations: Theory and practice* (3rd ed., pp. 26–46). Crows Nest, Australia: Allen & Unwin.

INDEX

© The Editor(s) (if applicable) and The Author(s) 2016   151
K. Fitch, *Professionalizing Public Relations*,
DOI 10.1057/978-1-137-57309-4